Specter's

What N

JAPAN

A Unique Travel Guide

Plan your travel with expert advice and Insider Tips: Travel confidently, Avoid Common Mistakes, and indulge in Art, Culture, History, Food, and nature.

Sarah Brekenridge

Table of Contents

Introduction..9

Chapter 1: Planning Your Trip to Japan........................11

Discovering Japan...11

Best Time to Visit Japan..................................... 12

Japan's Year-Round Appeal..................................13

Booking Essentials for Japan...............................14

Packing Essentials for Japan................................16

What to Avoid When Planning Trip to Japan...................17

Chapter 2: Savvy Traveler's Tips and Tricksaii...................20

Getting Around Japan....................................... 21

What NOT To Do While Travelling Around Japan........... 25

Staying Safe in Japan..27

Respectful Behavior and Cultural Etiquette......................28

What NOT To Do in Social Situations.............................. 29

Chapter 3: Tokyo and Kanto Region – Dos and Don'ts...... 33

Discovering Tokyo... 33

What to Do in Tokyo.. 34

What Events to Enjoy in Tokyo and Around...................45

What to Do in the Kanto Region....................................... 48

Where to Eat in Tokyo and the Kanto Region...................49

What to Eat in Tokyo and the Kanto Region 51

Where to Stay in Tokyo and the Kanto Region 53

What NOT to Do in Tokyo and the Kanto Region..............54

Chapter 4: Mount Fuji and Chubu Region – Dos and Don'ts..57

Discovering the Chubu Region.. 57

What to Do in the Chubu Region...................................... 58

What Events to Enjoy in the Chubu Region......................70

Where to Eat in the Chubu Region...................................71

What to Eat in the Chubu Region......................................72

Where to Stay in the Chubu Region..................................74

What NOT to Do in the Chubu Region..............................75

Chapter 5: Kyoto and Kansai Region – Dos and Don'ts.........72

Discovering Kyoto.. 77

What to Do in Kyoto... 78

What Events to Enjoy in Kyoto..85

Discovering the Kansai Region.. 86

What to Do in the Kansai Region......................................87

Where to Eat in Kyoto and the Kansai Region................90

What to Eat in Kyoto and the Kansai Region..................92

Where to Stay in Kyoto and the Kansai Region..............93

What NOT to Do in Kyoto and the Kansai Region...........94

Chapter 6: Hiroshima and the Chugoku Region – Dos and Don'ts... 96

Discovering Hiroshima.. 96

What to Do in Hiroshima... 97

What Events to Enjoy in Hiroshima...................................103

Discovering the Chugoku Region.......................................104

What to Do in the Chugoku Region....................................105

Where to Eat in Hiroshima and the Chugoku Region.........107

What to Eat in Hiroshima and the Chugoku Region...........108

Where to Stay in Hiroshima and the Chugoku Region..........110

What NOT to Do in Hiroshima and the Chugoku Region.....111

Chapter 7: The Tohuku Region – Dos and Don'ts...............113

Discovering the Tohuku Region.. 113

What to Do in the Tohuku Region..................................... 114

What Events to Enjoy in the Tohuku Region......................121

Where to Eat in the Tohuku Region...................................121

What to Eat in the Tohuku Region....................................123

Where to Stay in the Tohuku Region.................................124

What NOT to Do in the Tohuku Region.............................125

Chapter 8: Sapporo and the Hokkaido Region – Dos and Don'ts...127

Discovering the Hokkaido Region...................................... 127

What to Do in the Hokkaido Region................................... 128

What Events to Enjoy in the Hokkaido Region.....................133

Where to Eat in the Hokkaido Region.................................135

What to Eat in the Hokkaido Region..................................136

Where to Stay in the Hokkaido Region................................138

What NOT to Do in the Hokkaido Region............................139

Chapter 9: The Shikoku Region – Dos and Don'ts................140

Discovering the Shikoku Region..............................140

What to Do in the Shikoku Region.........................141

What Events to Enjoy in the Shikoku Region.........................148

Where to Eat in the Shikoku Region....................................149

What to Eat in the Shikoku Region..........................150

Where to Stay in the Shikoku Region.......................152

What NOT to Do in the Shikoku Region....................................153

Chapter 10: The Kyushu and Okinawa Region – Dos and Don'ts...154

Discovering the Kyushu and Okinawa Region..........................154

What to Do in the Kyushu and Okinawa Region.........................155

What Events to Enjoy in the Kyushu and Okinawa Region.........164

Where to Eat in the Kyushu and Okinawa Region......................165

What to Eat in the Kyushu and Okinawa Region.........................167

Where to Stay in the Kyushu and Okinawa Region....................168

What NOT to Do in the Kyushu and Okinawa Region.................170

Conclusion..171

Conclusion..172

References..173

Introduction

O f the thousands of countries you can visit worldwide, Japan can leave visitors in awe and delight through its perfect harmony of ancient customs and traditions that come together with modernity. What is so beautiful about Japan is that beyond its skyscrapers and bright lights, you'll see in the bustling cities its ability to preserve a sense of tranquility and order, reflecting its core values of finding harmony and balance. As you wander the streets of Japan, you'll find the roads perfectly coexist with centuries-old temples and shrines, creating a juxtaposition of past and present that makes Japan famous.

Beyond Japan's bustling cities, the country's landscapes show impressive diversity, from the snow-capped mountains of Hokkaido to the dense forest in Kyushu. Visiting these areas will also transport you back to ancient times and give you a sense of tranquility, peace, and admiration.

There is much to be said about Japan: the beautiful culture and hospitable people. But what would make you want to visit a country so far away from home? Going to a country with a different lifestyle can feel daunting, from its language to the typography. However, for such a big trip, it can be challenging to distinguish what you should do in Japan to ensure you gain the most authentic experience versus the tourist traps that lack historical or cultural significance. Knowing how rich Japan's culture is, you want to find and explore the lesser-known historical sites and villages and experience the unique hospitality Japan offers from its accommodations and restaurants.

But first, it comes down to researching and planning. If you've already begun this part, you've probably found a plethora of information on Japan that feels overwhelming, but the first order of travel business is getting there. The traveling aspect alone likely feels daunting and full of obstacles as you try to navigate the logistical elements of booking your flights and accommodations ahead of time and arranging the ways you want to get around the country. This, along with trying to make an itinerary that prioritizes the important sites to see and allocating enough time for each place, also poses its challenges. Additionally, the plethora of information out there can create confusion as you try to maximize your experience while sticking to the budget you have set.

As someone who has been to Japan, I learned a number of tricks that made the experience fulfilling. In this book, we'll explore the many cities and villages and also highlight some of the things to avoid. This book will be an excellent starting point for your research as there will be detailed information on the attractions and what to expect to spend at each. By reading this book, you'll be able to narrow down what you want to do in Japan, gain a deeper understanding of their customs, practice cultural sensitivity, and make the choices that will best fit your trip.

Whether you are returning to Japan or going for the first time, this will be a trip of a lifetime and one that will leave you talking about it for years to come.

Chapter 1:

Planning Your Trip to Japan

*J*apan is the most intoxicating place for me. In Kyoto, there's an inn called the Tawaraya, which is quite extraordinary. The Japanese culture fascinates me: the food, the dress, the manners, and the traditions. It's the travel experience that has moved me the most.
—Roman Coppola

Discovering Japan

Along the eastern edge of Asia is Japan, a country comprising four main islands—Hokkaido, Honshu, Shikoku, and Kyushu—among 4,000 other small islands. As you have learned, this fantastic country is beautifully harmonious, blending its well-preserved ancient customs with modern life.

Japan's history goes back at least 30,000 years. Long before it became an archipelago, the country was connected to Siberia and Korea by land, making it accessible on foot. About 12,000 years ago, the first settlers to create a society in

Japan were called the Jamons. Some settlers, known as the Ainu people, also arrived by boat and settled in Japan simultaneously. These two groups lived together, hunting, fishing, and foraging plants until 300, when the Yayoi arrived from Korea and China and settled on Honshu Island.

By 660, Japan had its first emperor, marking the start of emperors over the next six centuries until the shoguns (military rulers) ruled the country from 1185 until 1868, when a new constitutional monarchy took over, ending the shoguns' rule. To date, Japan still has a constitutional monarchy led by an emperor.

Beyond the exciting history you will learn about on your trip, you'll see plenty of centuries-old streets, ancient temples, and tranquil gardens that will bring peace to your trip. Beyond the cities, Mount Fuji and its dramatic peak are also iconic symbols of Japan's natural beauty and will leave you in awe.

Whatever is bringing you to Japan, there is so much to see and uncover. It all starts with planning your trip, though. So, let's get into the basics of preparing for your trip to Japan.

Best Time to Visit Japan

Choosing the right time to visit Japan will depend on your preferences and what you want to see and do. Japan's climate and seasonal attractions change throughout the year, which should also be considered while planning your trip.

One of the key factors to consider is that Japan sees all four seasons, each offering its own charm. Spring is one of the most beautiful and popular times to visit Japan (between March and May) as the mild weather is pleasant for being outside and enjoying the sites. Naturally, one of the most popular attractions for people to visit Japan in the spring is to see the cherry blossoms (sakura) blooming, transforming parks and streets into a stunning sea of pink. While the cherry blossom trees traditionally bloom in the spring months, you can see them as early as January if you're visiting one of the southern islands, such as Okinawa. Either way, it's a magical time for those who deeply appreciate nature and want to capture some great photos, especially if you attend a hanami (flower-viewing) festival. In terms of temperatures, they range between 35 °F and 75 °F during the spring.

Summer in Japan starts with plenty of rain. However, by July and August, it tends to become quite hot and humid, bringing many people to the beaches to swim and cool off or hike the mountains to see a different perspective from high up in the sky. Temperatures tend to range between 60 °F and 86 °F. Japan's summer months also have two iconic festivals: the Japanese Festival (matsuri) and the fireworks (hanabi taikai). At the matsuri, there are plenty of opportunities to immerse yourself in Japanese culture, from traditional dancing to games and music. The fireworks are also an enjoyable event, especially as this is a tradition that goes back a few centuries.

By autumn's arrival in Japan in September, the foliage changes to vibrant gold, red, and amber colors. This is an ideal time to visit if you prefer mild-to-cooler temperatures and want to appreciate the natural scenery differently. Visiting Japan between September and November is a perfect time for drives through the countryside landscapes, visits to the smaller Japanese villages, and leisurely strolls through the beautiful gardens. As the temperatures cool down, they're usually between 44 °F and 63 °F.

Winter in Japan offers a completely different experience. The season begins in December, and while it is much colder (between 21 °F and 54 °F, the snowy landscapes create postcard-perfect scenes, especially in Hokkaido and the Japanese Alps. This is a great time to visit if you love skiing and snowboarding or want to enjoy the hot springs (rotenburo) in Sapporo or Nagasaki.

Aside from what you can expect to experience in terms of weather patterns, one thing to be mindful of is that Japan does see a number of typhoons, primarily between July and October. If a typhoon were to land in Japan, remember to be mindful of the warnings provided for your safety.

Japan's Year-Round Appeal

As you consider which season is best for you to visit Japan, consider a few things:

- Do you mind hot or cold weather?
- Do you hate crowded areas?
- Do you want to spend a significant amount of time outdoors?

Spring

With spring bringing the blossoming of the cherry blossoms and starting to thaw out the cold wintery days, visiting the country between March and May is ideal for enjoying picturesque settings and outdoor activities, such as hiking, biking, and exploring historical sites. However, because of the cherry blossom season, spring is also the peak tourist season for Japan. Therefore, you can expect more crowds and higher prices for accommodations and flights.

Summer

Summer is also a peak tour season for Japan as it invites travelers to experience the many festivals and events. The warmer weather also appeals to those wishing to partake in outdoor activities and enjoy the beaches. Of course, this may not be the season to go if you don't love hot and humid weather. It's also likely that you could experience travel interruptions due to a typhoon.

Autumn

While autumn brings cooler temperatures, a change of scenery among the trees, and different cultural festivals, this season still tends to be a bit busier. However, flights and accommodation pricing have started to become a little cheaper.

Winter

Winter in Japan offers stunning scenery. However, it can be particularly chilly, especially in the country's northern regions. However, it makes for great winter sports, and Mount Fuji is stunning to see as it is covered with snow. Also, accommodation and flights are cheaper because it's not as touristy as you would find in spring to mid-autumn.

Booking Essentials for Japan

As you plan your trip to Japan, you want to consider all of the essentials to make it the trip of a lifetime. Aside from considering the seasons and crowds, you'll also want to consider your flights, where you want to stay, and if you wish to join any tour companies to make your itinerary planning seamless.

Flights to Japan

Japan has several international airports throughout the country, making it seamless to arrive in Japan from the US. The primary entry points into Japan are in Tokyo at the Narita International Airport and the Haneda Airport, which offer easy access to the city and connect flights to other parts of the country. Some of the other major international airports include Kansai International Airport in Osaka, which can give you easy access to the Kansai Region, and Chubu Centrair International Airport in Nagoya, which will provide you with easy access to the Chubu region and central parts of the country.

The main airlines that will take you to Japan are

- American Airlines
- Japan Airlines
- All Nippon Airways
- Hawaiian Airlines
- Singapore Airlines
- Delta Air Lines

- United Airlines

When booking your flights, the next thing to consider is if you want to find direct flights or if you're okay with a layover. Remember, flying to Japan takes you halfway around the globe, so the flight will be long. While direct flights that skip the layovers may be convenient, they can also be more expensive. It's also a good idea to book your flights at least six months in advance to ensure you get the best rate. Book your flights eight months in advance to ensure you secure the best possible rate if you plan to go during peak season. It's always best to keep an alert for flight research; Google Flights is an excellent option. You can also contact a travel consultant to help you find the best pricing or book your flights directly through the airline to ensure you get the best service should something happen.

Visa Requirements and Documentation

For US citizens, if you will be in Japan for up to 90 days, you only need a valid passport to access the country. Your passport must have at least six months of validity. When you arrive in Japan, you may need to provide fingerprint scans and be photographed.

Travel Insurance

Travel insurance, while not mandatory, is always advisable for traveling in the event something happens. When purchasing travel insurance, it's important to read the fine print as you want travel insurance that will cover

- medical expenses (including unexpected illnesses or injuries)
- cancellations of trip delays
- lost or stolen baggage
- flight interruption

Accommodation

There are plenty of accommodation options throughout Japan, but it is wise to consider what you feel you'll need for a comfortable stay. Remember, you're not spending days on end in your accommodation, but you want something that will provide comfort and relaxation after a day of exploring. The other thing to consider is what will suit your budget. If you wish for an iconic experience, you should consider staying at least one to two nights in a traditional Japanese inn (ryokan) with the futons on the floor. However, there are modern hotels, hostels, guesthouses, apartments, capsule hotels, and other unique stays like temple lodgings and minshuku (family immersion experiences).

Staying in the major cities, like Tokyo, Osaka, and Kyoto, as well as the central districts, including Shinjuku, Shibuya, and Namba, have easy access to famous landmarks, shopping districts, and restaurants. We will explore the transportation options in the next chapter, but this is good to know when you start booking your accommodations, especially if you're not planning on renting a car.

Lastly, accommodations vary and could include Wi-Fi access, complimentary breakfast, on-site restaurants, communal areas, and traditional Japanese baths (onsen). You may also want to consider the layout and size of the rooms and what will suit your comfort level, as some space may be limited. The earlier you research and book your accommodations, the better the chances you will find something that will work for you.

Activities and Tours

It's understandable if you want someone to take care of the itinerary, deepen your knowledge of the country, and give you a more immersive experience for your trip, so you may want to consider booking a tour. There are several tour companies in Japan that can help you with that. Some offer one-day tours, and others provide multiday tours. You should be looking for tour operators who specialize in Japanese travel and have in-depth knowledge of Japanese culture, history, and landmarks. If you're looking at a tour company that offers multiday tours, you'll want to consider what destinations will be covered, transportation, accommodations, if it is group or self-guided, and the different experiences within the package. These considerations will help you build your itinerary to ensure you see everything you want to see in Japan.

Packing Essentials for Japan

Chances are, you won't be in Japan for just a week—you will probably be there for a minimum of 14 days. The basic thing to remember is the season you're going in. You'll want some warm layers if you're going in the spring or autumn. If you're going in the summer, you will want light and breathable clothes. In winter, you'll want heavier layers to keep the chill-out. The next thing to keep in mind is packing light—but how?

Compressible packing cubes will be your best friend when it comes to packing. They will allow you to organize your outfits by day so that you don't need to rummage around in your suitcase. One of the greatest tricks for packing your compressible packing cubes is to pack things you can mix and match over two to three days and then label them. In terms of what types of clothing, you can get away with casual clothes. Japan is quite well-known for its eclectic fashion. So, if you're a jeans and T-shirt person, you'll be fine. You should also wear shoes that you can slip on and off easily, especially if you're staying in a ryokan or going to a restaurant where you must remove your shoes. (However, it's also considered rude to be barefoot, so if you're wearing sandals, be sure to have a pair of socks on you!)

In addition to your clothing options, some other essential things to pack include

- toiletries in travel-sized bottles
- sunscreen
- a hat, scarf, and gloves (for the cooler months)
- sunglasses
- other personal care items
- a reusable water bottle
- a phrasebook
- a universal adaptor

Japan's Currency

Japan's currency is the yen (¥). While much of the country, especially major cities, accept credit cards for payments, many establishments only accept cash or prefer cash for smaller purchases or admission fees. It's always better to pick up your currency at a currency exchange store or through your bank before your trip. Typically, exchange rates are higher at airports, making exchanging cash more expensive, and not every ATM will accept cards that are not from Japan unless you go to a Seven Bank ATM found in 7-Eleven or Japan Post ATMs. For larger purchases, it's better to use your credit card as it can guarantee the best exchange rate, for example, at restaurants, hotels, and department or convenience store purchases.

One thing to keep in mind about the yen is that the currency exchange, compared to the US and Canada, is relatively cheap. Prices will be listed throughout this book for the main attractions to help you with your budget, but even the food can be as low as around $6.

What to Avoid When Planning Your Trip to Japan

In addition to helping you plan your trip, this book also covers everything you should avoid while in Japan. These sections will help you plan your trip better and be prepared for what to expect when visiting this beautiful country.

Don't Forget to Plan Ahead

During the peak seasons, Japan sees a lot of travelers coming to the country. As such, the accommodations and attractions can be booked up pretty quickly. So, if you plan on visiting during peak season, start booking your accommodations and attractions as soon as possible.

Don't Overload Your Itinerary

Throughout this book, you will learn about the many things you can see, do, and experience in Japan. Even if you're in the country for three months, the chances of you getting through everything will not likely happen. Manage your expectations and remember that even having easy-going days can be just as immersive as seeing famous landmarks.

Don't Overlook Langauge Barrier

English is not widely spoken in Japan, especially outside major tourist areas. Consider learning some basic Japanese phrases or using translation apps to communicate with locals.

Don't Underestimate Japan's Weather

Given that Japan has four seasons, each comes with its own weather patterns and conditions. This is crucial, especially if you plan to immerse yourself in outdoor activities where the microclimates vary. Additionally, given the country's location on our planet, it's also prone to natural disasters, including typhoons, earthquakes, and tsunamis. It's always best to be aware of any natural disaster and weather warnings should they come up during your trip.

Don't Just Stay at Western-style hotels.

Western-style hotels may offer some comfort, but they won't give you an authentic Japanese experience. Remember, you won't get to travel to Japan every day. Look at other unique options, like staying at a temple or a minshuku, to immerse yourself in Japanese culture and cultivate your understanding of their way of life.

Don't Forget the Right Adaptors

Japan uses power sockets like we do: type A, which fits two-prong plugs, and type B, which fits all plugs. However, not every place will have a type B socket, so it's best to pack a universal travel adapter to ensure you can use your electronics as needed. You should also ensure the adapter you buy can convert power to avoid frying your devices (primarily an electric shaver or a hair styling tool).

Don't Overindulge in Paid Attractions

While paid attractions may seem to be the only thing you should do in Japan, they can quickly eat up your budget! They also won't all provide the cultural immersion you may be seeking, and they'll be crowded during the busier travel seasons. That's not to say that they are all bad, of course. However, don't forget to check out the free attractions to visit too.

Don't Assume Everything Is Expensive

Many people who are considering traveling to Japan assume everything will be expensive. While you could spend a lot of money in this country, if you know where to go and start making a budget now, the trip won't cost you a fortune.

Don't Only Visit During Cherry Blossom Season

Cherry blossom season is one of the most appealing reasons people travel to Japan. But even after the cherry blossoms have bloomed, there is still plenty of beautiful scenery to enjoy, especially in the many gardens around Japan! Remember, this season is particularly busy, so if you don't want to be stuck in crowds, be open and flexible to travel another time of the year.

Don't Limit Your Experiences to the Major Cities

It may feel tempting to stick to the major cities, but there is beauty beyond the hustle and bustle. Be open to exploring other Japanese towns and villages as you'll be able to immerse yourself deeper in the culture and see a different way of life.

Don't Rely Solely on Google Map

While Google Maps is useful for navigation, it may not always provide accurate information in Japan, especially in rural areas. Consider carrying physical maps as a backup.

Be careful about what kind of clothes you are carrying

Japan has conservative dress standards, especially in religious sites and traditional settings. Avoid revealing clothing and dress modestly, especially when visiting temples and shrines.

Don't forget to carry some cash.

While credit cards are accepted in many places, cash is still king in Japan, especially in smaller establishments and rural areas. Make sure to have enough yen on hand for your trip.

Chapter 2:

Savvy Traveler's Tips and Tricks

Japan was closed for just under 1,000 days when it finally reopened for post-pandemic tourism. Naturally, many were itching to jet-set elsewhere to explore different cultures, bask in the sun, or reunite with long-distance relatives. While Europe and the United Kingdom are some of the top places people want to travel to, Japan has also topped that list, according to Gillett (2023).

More interestingly, the people wanting to visit the country the most are Gen Z and Millennials. Why do these particular generations want to visit Japan? Pop culture is one of those reasons, and so is Japan's cuisine and unique experiences. No matter your age, there will always be something that will appeal to your inner adventurous self. But of course, with Japan being on several islands and having dense populations in the major cities, how do you get around to experience everything Japan has to offer? In this chapter, we will dive into how you can get around Japan and how to stay safe and adapt to their cultural standards to ensure you can blend in rather than experience a culture shock on your trip.

Getting Around Japan

Understanding how to get around Japan is imperative for your trip so that you can fully experience everything the country has to offer. While Japan is an archipelago, the country has a highly efficient and interconnected transportation system, including bullet trains (shinkansen), local trains, buses, subways, planes, and ferries. Learning to navigate the many transportation networks ensures seamless travel between cities and grants access to hidden gems off the beaten path and away from the hustle and bustle.

Subways in Japan

Japan's subway system is one of the best ways to get around if you're staying in any of these major cities:

- Tokyo
- Osaka
- Kyoto
- Fukuoka
- Kobe
- Yokohama
- Nagoya
- Sendai

They have been making improvements over the years to provide multilingual support to make it easier for travelers to navigate the rail system. However, you may notice that some subway stations are close to one another in similar regions of cities. Therefore, when navigating the subway system, it's advisable to double-check the subway maps to see which trains will take you to your destination since changing lines can be expensive. If you're looking to save money, it's wise to pick up a one-day or two-day pass. You may also want to pick up a Welcome Suica Card that is designated for tourism and expires 28 days after the day of activation. This reloadable card allows you to use it on subways, taxis, monorails, shopping, and dining. This card is rechargeable as well.

The Rail System

Japan's rail systems are some of the best in the world for their efficiency, speed, and coverage of the country—an impressive 19,029 miles to be exact—making them an indispensable part of travel within the country. The bullet train is one of the backbones of getting between destinations in what seems like a flash, but even the local railways have their charm, bringing you through scenic villages, mountains, and countryside.

If you are exploring Tokyo and the surrounding suburbs, you will want to pick up the Greater Tokyo Pass. This pass will give you unlimited rides on 13 of Kanto's private railway lines, the 31 bus companies around the suburbs, and within Tokyo for five days. There is also an unlimited railway pass you can buy which is good for up to three days, giving you access to the 13 railway lines.

Greater Tokyo Pass

Pass type	Adult	Children
Five days	¥7,200	¥3,600
Three days	¥6,000	¥3,000

Bus Travel

Bus travel in Japan is an alternative and cost-effective way to travel. Several options include local city buses, sightseeing buses tailored to specific tourist attractions, long-distance highway buses, and overnight buses.

Your Welcome Suico card and Japan Rail Pass should cover most of your transportation costs for local buses. However, if you are opting to take a highway bus or overnight bus, you'll need to purchase those tickets separately, or you can buy one of these bus passes, which will give you access to a number of the different companies:

- **Japan Bus Pass**: The Japan Bus Pass is an excellent option for those looking to stick to a tighter budget. This pass is good to choose if you're okay with sleeping on a bus for the night. These passes are available for three, five, or seven days and do not need to be used consecutively.
- **Tohoku Highway Bus Ticket**: With the Tohoku Highway Bus Ticket, you will have unlimited access to over 100 highway and local bus lines in the Tohoku region for two or three consecutive days.

- **Sun Q Pass:** The Sun Q Pass gives you unlimited travel on local and highway buses in Kyushu for three or four consecutive days. This pass has two options: the All Kyushu pass and the Southern Kyushu pass.
- **Hokkaido Budget Bus Pass:** The Hokkaido Budget Bus Pass will give you unlimited travel on select Hokkaido bus routes for three or five consecutive days. There are two versions of this pass: One that will cover the entire Hokkaido region and the other that sticks to the central areas, including Asahikawa and Sapporo.
- **Shoryudo Bus Pass:** If you're in the Chubu, Nagoya, Takayama, Shirakawago, or Kanazawa regions, the Shoryudo Bus Bass will give you access to unlimited rides on highway and local buses for three or five consecutive days.

Domestic Flights

Domestic air travel in Japan is another convenient and efficient way to get around the country. The main airlines that fly domestically around the country are Japan Airlines and All Nippon Airways. However, you can also book domestic flights with these airlines:

- Skymark Airlines
- Peach Aviation
- Jetstar Japan
- Air Do
- Starflyer
- Solaseed Air
- Fuji Dream Airlines
- IBEX Airlines
- Spring Japan

Ferry Services

If you have time and want to experience the scenery of Japan from the water, the ferry services in Japan will give you a unique mode of transportation while connecting you to various islands and coastal regions across the country. While taking the ferry, you can enjoy breathtaking views of the Pacific Ocean, Seto Inland Sea, and other picturesque waterways between your destinations. The crossings can be short or long to connect you to different parts of Japan and remote areas like Okinawa and Hokkaido.

The Japan Rail Pass does cover some of the ferry services. However, it is best to verify which lines it covers, which can be done through their website.

Taxis and Ride Services

Taxis and ride-share services are readily available in the major cities and the countryside to take you to various points of interest. However, while they are convenient and handy if you are traveling with more than two people, they are also the most expensive option compared to other modes of transportation. Fares are calculated by a running meter, and a surcharge will be added if you take a taxi between 10 p.m. and 5 a.m. Most city taxis take credit cards unless you're taking a cab in the countryside, where they will only accept cash.

If you plan to use a taxi to get from an airport, they are available with fixed fares; you will just want to ask the driver before you hop in, as the fares vary between zones.

Uber is another option available in Japan. Of course, with Uber, you will just need to change your location in the app so it can charge you accordingly.

Cycling in Japan

Cycling in Japan will offer a unique and immersive way to experience the country's rich cultural heritage, beautiful landscapes, and vibrant cultural centers. Japan has plenty of well-maintained bike paths, designated cycling routes, and bike-friendly infrastructures, which make cycling in this country a breeze. You can rent bicycles easily from bike shops, tourist offices, or hotels if they offer the service and are generally cash only. If the tourist offices or hotels don't offer the service, they can point you in the right direction. There are also bike-share companies in major cities that will make it easy to pick up and drop off at different points around the city. If you use these bike-for-hire options, they will accept major international credit cards.

Before setting out, especially in the countryside, it's wise to familiarize yourself with local laws and cycling etiquette, such as riding on the left side of the road, obeying traffic signals, and yielding to pedestrians. It is the same courtesy you would give back home, but cycling is big in Japan, and it will be a great way to blend in with fellow cyclists on the paths and roads.

Renting a Car or Motorcycle

Renting a car or motorcycle while in Japan will give you the freedom and flexibility to explore Japan without having to depend on timetables for buses and trains and other ways to get to the country's more remote regions or hidden gems. You can rent vehicles from rental agencies or at the airport. However, before your trip, you must obtain an international driving permit, which you can get through the American Automobile Association (AAA). When you pick up your rental car, you must have this documentation alongside your valid driver's license. You must also be at least 18 years old. As always, you should take a video of the car before you drive off to ensure all marks and dents (if any) are recorded.

Before your trip, it's advisable to familiarize yourself with Japan's traffic regulations, road signs, and driving customs. For example, Japan drives on the left side of the road and hardly displays any aggressive driving. When driving in city areas, the speed is 24 mph, 18 mph on city streets, and between 50 to 62 mph on highways. Otherwise, the speed is generally 31 to 37 mph. Additionally, you should be aware of toll roads, which accept cash, credit cards, and electronic toll collection (ETC). If you are on a toll road, ensure you are in the lane that accepts cash and credit cards.

What Not to Do While Traveling Around Japan

Try to avoid Rush Hour

Japan's rush hour can be extremely crowded, especially in major cities like Tokyo and Osaka. Try to avoid traveling during peak hours to minimize stress and discomfort.

Don't Forget to Purchase an IC Card

IC cards like Suica and Pasmo are convenient for traveling on trains, buses, and subways in Japan. Purchase one upon arrival and load it with credit for hassle-free transportation.

Don't Forget to Carry Slip-on Shoes

There's a decent chance you'll need to remove your shoes when you're out and about. Shoes are always removed when entering someone's home, but also in some restaurants, shrines, temples, and attractions. Japanese people have perfected the art of slipping into and out of shoes while barely even crouching down, so its important that you carry low-maintenance slip-on shoes and clean, hole-free socks.

Don't Eat on Public Transportation

Unless you're taking a long train ride, it's best to avoid eating an entire meal while riding subways and local buses. It's better to eat a small snack than something that can leave a mess or make a ton of noise.

Don't Use the Extra Seat for Your Bags

It may feel tempting to place your bag on the seat next to you (especially if a train is empty), but don't do this. It's seen as rude, and someone may want that seat.

Additionally, putting large luggage on the floor is not advisable as it can be a tripping hazard. If you're on the subways, try to keep your bag on your lap or stow it beneath your seat. If you're on a local train, use the racks above to stow away your bag.

Don't Expect Cell Service in Remote Areas

Cell service is excellent in urban areas; however, service may be spotty in Japan's countryside and other remote regions. Ensure you download directions on your smartphone to avoid getting lost, especially since GPS in remote areas can also lose its signal.

Don't Forget to Carry Tissues

Many public restrooms in Japan do not provide toilet paper, so it's a good idea to carry tissues or a small pack of tissues with you for emergencies.

Don't Forget About Women-Only Cars

Depending on the time of day you travel, some trains have cars reserved for women only. A large pink sticker on the floor of the door indicates when these times occur.

Don't Forget to Get a Japan Rail Pass

The Japan Rail Pass (JR Pass) is a special ticket available for tourists that allows unlimited travel on most of Japan's railways, including the bullet trains (shinkansen), limited express trains, ferries, monorails, and local JR lines for a set period (7, 14, or 21 days of travel). This pass gives you the flexibility and convenience to explore Japan without buying individual tickets for each trip.

When you go to pick up your JR Pass, you will notice that there are two types: blue and green. The blue pass is your standard economy pass, and the green is the first-class version, which allows you to enjoy your journey in a quieter setting. However, this pass will not cover the subway systems, so ensure you pick up a Welcome Suica card for that travel!

You can purchase the pass online before you go. However, you can also pick it up at any Japan Rail train station at the green window.

Blue Pass: Standard

Duration	Adult	Child (6 - 11 yr old)
7 days	¥50,000	¥25,000
14 days	¥80,000	¥40,000

Green Pass: First Class

Duration	Adult	Child (6 - 11 yr old)
7 days	¥70,000	¥35,000
14 days	¥110,000	¥55,000

Staying Safe in Japan

Of all the countries in the world you can visit, Japan has the lowest crime levels. In fact, theft is almost a rare event. However, while you may see people leave their belongings unattended momentarily, it's still wise to be aware of your surroundings to ensure you don't fall victim to petty theft. Should you need assistance from the police, there are small police boxes, known as a koban, in the neighborhoods.

Other risks that are more likely in Japan are natural disasters (but that shouldn't deter you from visiting the country). Japan is susceptible to earthquakes since the archipelago is near four large tectonic plates. Additionally, it sees its fair share of typhoons and wet weather. Knowing the prevalence of natural disasters and the destruction that can come with them, Japan has built infrastructures to minimize the damage. You'll be fine if you listen to warnings and forecasts.

Emergency and Assistance

Emergency Numbers

Should you ever need emergency assistance, keep these numbers in mind:

- Police: 110
- Fire or ambulance: 119
- Metropolitan Police in Tokyo: 03-3501-0110

They also have an English line available 24 hours a day all year round.

Japan National Tourism Organization (JNTO) Information Center in Tokyo: 03-3201-3331

This line is available between 9 a.m. and 5 p.m. daily.

If you need to contact the U.S. Embassy, it is in Tokyo at 1-10-5 Akasaka, Minato-ku, Tokyo 107-8420. Their phone number is 03-3224-5000.

Respectful Behavior and Cultural Etiquette

Respectful behavior and cultural etiquette ensure a positive and enriching experience for Japanese locals and travelers.

Interacting With the Locals

In Japan, there is a high value on harmony, politeness, and mutual respect. By observing proper etiquette, such as bowing when you greet others (especially hosts at inns or guesthouses), removing shoes when entering homes or certain establishments (such as temples), and using phrases such as Gomen nasai (I'm sorry) or sumimasen (excuse me), you will be able to demonstrate respect for Japanese culture and foster positive interactions with locals.

Bathing Etiquette

If you intend to experience a bathhouse at least once in Japan, this practice is deeply ingrained in Japanese culture and holds significant importance for locals and visitors. Therefore, whether you intend to enjoy the soothing waters at an onsen (traditional hot spring) or will be bathing in a sento (communal bathhouse), it is essential to adhere to proper etiquette to ensure a respectful bathing experience for you and those around you. Additionally, if you have tattoos, you should inquire about the establishment's policy beforehand, as some traditional hot springs and bathhouses may have restrictions.

Upon entering the bathing area, it is customary to thoroughly wash and rinse your body at the provided shower stations before entering the communal bathing area. Don't be alarmed to see others nude; this is the norm in these establishments. However, it is also essential to maintain modesty by using a small bath towel to cover private areas when you walk between the shower and the bath. While in the bath area, respectful behavior, such as not talking loudly or splashing water, will maintain a tranquil and relaxing atmosphere. When you are done, rinse any remaining soap and thoroughly dry yourself with a towel before leaving the bathing area, as it promotes cleanliness.

Historical and Sacred Sites

Visiting temples and other historical sites in Japan will offer you a deeper insight into the country's cultural heritage and spiritual traditions. Thousands of temples, shrines, and United Nations Educational, Scientific and Cultural Organization (UNESCO) World Heritage sites are scattered across the country, allowing you to explore the intricate and interesting architecture and find peace and tranquility in the gardens and other sacred areas.

When you visit temples and shrines, you must respect and honor their significance. Before entering the temples, placing a coin in the offering box is customary, followed by a small prayer. You may also be required to remove your shoes and put them on shoe racks by the entrance; alternatively, if the temple provides them, you can place them in a plastic bag and bring them with you. If you are wearing sandals, ensure you have a pair of clean socks. If you visit a shrine, you may be required to cleanse your hands and mouth at a purification fountain. Any unused water can be disposed of next to the fountain. It is not mandatory to do this, but it is a great way to immerse yourself in the sacred experience. Participating in other rituals, such as bowing or lighting incense, can deepen your cultural understanding and foster a spiritual connection.

If you want to take photos at temples or shrines, you should be able to do so on the grounds. However, it's mostly prohibited inside the buildings. When in doubt, always look for signage or ask a staff member.

Dining and Culinary Etiquette

When you visit restaurants, it's often customary to receive a small towel to wipe your hands before eating. Don't use this to wipe your face or neck; it will be seen as impolite. When you receive your meal, use the phrase Itadakimasu, which means "I humbly receive," to express your gratitude for the meal and those who spent the time creating it for you. You also do not need to leave a tip, as it is uncommon in Japan. The prices presented for meals are believed to be fair, and if you tip, it may be considered rude.

Chopsticks are a common way to eat meals. However, not everyone is a pro at using chopsticks, so you may ask for a utensil (but it may not be available). If you order soup, such as miso soup, it is traditionally drunk directly out of the bowl. You will be given a soup spoon if the soup comes in a larger bowl. Also, you can slurp the noodles (some believe it even enhances the flavor!)

What Not to Do in Social Situations

Don't Be Loud or Display Disruptive Behavior in Public Places

One of the things you may notice in Japan is that it's a relatively quiet country, even in major cities. Therefore, be mindful of your volume level no matter where you are to ensure you respect the environment and contribute to a tranquil space. Also, don't watch videos or make phone calls while on public transit.

Don't Wear Shoes Inside Homes

Don't be surprised by the number of shoes you see at the door of various establishments. This is one of the customs Japan is well-known for. If you are required to take off your shoes, especially if you stay at a Japanese home or inn, you will be provided with indoor slippers. Some may even give you different slippers to wear in the bathrooms. This ancient tradition dates back to the year 700 and ensures cleanliness.

Another custom when removing your shoes is to redirect them to face the door. This makes it easy for you to slip back on when leaving.

Don't Use Chopsticks Incorrectly

When you pull apart your wooden chopsticks, ensure you don't rub them to remove splinters. This may be customary in the US and Canada, but you won't see a Japanese person doing this (and they may look at you with an odd look). Also, it is frowned upon to pass food between chopsticks. This is due to a funeral ritual where the bones of the loved one are passed following the cremation ceremony. Another thing you should not do with your chopsticks is stand them up in a rice bowl. This is also a funeral ritual where incense is placed in rice.

Don't Skip Lines

If there is one thing Japan does well, it is its queues. Don't skip these, especially if boarding a train or bus. Waiting patiently in line ensures everyone who needs to get off the train or bus can do so and then follow people onto the train in an orderly fashion.

Don't Show Public Displays of Affection

Public displays of affection (PDA) may be something we see at home, but the Japanese are private people and won't kiss or hug in public. The most they will do is hold hands. So, be mindful of how much PDA you do.

Don't Blow Your Nose in Public

If you are sniffling, you should blow your nose rather than make the annoying sniffle sound or consistently wipe your nose on your sleeve. However, considering Japan is quiet, blowing your nose is considered rude as it disrupts the quiet; plus, there is the factor of no garbage on the subways or at your restaurant table. If you need to blow your nose, find a place without disrupting others or dab your nose with a tissue. On that particular note about runny noses, if you do have a cold, it's common to wear a mask to prevent the virus from spreading around.

Don't Walk and Eat

While there are a number of food vendors on the streets, you will never see a local grab a bite to eat and keep walking. They will grab it and find a place in a designated area to eat and enjoy it as a sign of appreciation and to avoid littering. Additionally, if you decide to grab something and continue walking, you'll be stuck carrying your garbage with you as there are not as many trash cans along the streets. If you pick food up from a street vendor, you are encouraged to be like a local and eat in a designated area, then continue with your ventures.

Don't Wear a Swimsuit at an Onsen or Sento

Unless you are visiting a co-ed or family-friendly onsen or sento, the baths are separated by gender and, therefore, require you to be naked. It may seem intimidating, but this ritual dates back centuries. It's an experience, and you may not find it weird when you realize everyone else is naked, too.

Don't Tip in Japan

Tipping is not customary in Japan and may be seen as rude. Appreciate the service you receive without the need for monetary rewards.

Don't Douse Your Rice in Soy Sauce

Rice is a starchy staple in Japan, and little bowls of sticky white grains are served for breakfast, lunch, and dinner there. Contrary to Western tastes, however, Japanese don't pour soy sauce directly onto their rice. You'll be looked at as aghast if you soak your bowl with salty sauce like a condiment topping (it would be akin to pouring sugar on your french fries or something equally odd). Rice is meant to balance out the flavors of other delectables on the table. If you must, you can dip a morsel of rice into a little side dish of soy or other sauces in your spread to give it a flavor boost. But don't douse the bowl directly, or you'll raise the eyebrows of your Japanese dining companions. Feel free to pour soy sauce directly on top of tofu, but not rice.

Don't Be Afraid to Slurp and Burp

With all these Japanese guidelines for table manners, it can take foreign visitors by surprise to hear the locals devouring their meals in a way we might consider a bit gauche. They'll sip, slurp, smack, suck, chew, chomp, and even burp audibly throughout the meal as a polite sign that they are enjoying the feast. The louder the better, it seems. So go ahead, forget what your mom taught you, and make a little gusto noise at a Japanese table. The cook will be flattered.

Don't Pour Your Own Drink

Alcohol is a key part of socializing in Japan, and the custom is for colleagues and friends to keep each others' glasses full and bottomless. This means there will be a constant stream of refills as everyone tries to top each other up. As a foreigner, you may be the beneficiary of this hospitable gesture more than most. So be careful; it can be challenging to keep tabs on how much you're imbibing here! Don't forget to reciprocate the gesture to others. The most polite and honorable way is to pour using two hands.

Avoid the Number Four

Four is a very superstitious number in Japan, sort of akin to the unlucky 13. The number four is pronounced shi in Japanese, which has the same sound as their word for death. There's actually an alternate pronunciation for this number, yon, so you can try to avoid these bad luck connotations. You'll often find four is skipped on room, floor or seat numbers in Japan. Nine is another unlucky number in Japan they go out of their way to avoid, as kyu sounds like their word for torture or suffering.

Don't talk on your Cell Phone Excessively.

Japan is one of the most densely populated countries in the world and has 90% penetration when it comes to mobile devices. You'd think they'd all be yammering on cell phones all day long. However, that's not the case. While almost everyone has a smartphone, there are some socially agreed upon etiquette rules for talking on them in public. The Japanese put group needs ahead of the individual, so they never want their phone usage to be considered a nuisance to others. They find it rude to talk loudly on the phone on the streets, on trains, on buses, or in other public spaces in Japan.

First Stop: Tokyo and the Kanto Region

In this chapter, we discussed everything you need to know about getting around Japan, how to keep yourself safe while traveling, and the cultural behavior and etiquette to follow in the country. You should now feel confident about interacting with the locals in Japan to ensure you don't stick out like a tourist.

Now that we have the basics covered, it's time to dive into Japan and everything the country offers. The first stop is Tokyo and the Kanto region, one of the most well-known areas of Japan.

Chapter 3:

Tokyo and Kanto Region—Dos and Don'ts

Discovering Tokyo

When many think of Tokyo, the most iconic images that come to mind are its bright city lights and bustling city atmosphere. This city is the capital of Japan, but its bright and modern metropolis, which we know today, goes back centuries. You can discover this through its cultural attractions, including the Shinjuku Gyoen National Garden and the famous Shibuya Crossing. Tokyo's unique character is also reflected in its themed cafes, including one with a Super Mario theme and another with an Alice in Wonderland theme. Beyond its quirks and distinctive neighborhoods, Tokyo's energy is electric, and visiting this iconic city will give you an unforgettable cultural experience.

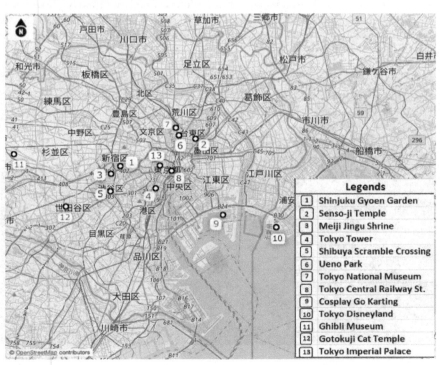

Legends
1 Shinjuku Gyoen Garden
2 Senso-ji Temple
3 Meiji Jingu Shrine
4 Tokyo Tower
5 Shibuya Scramble Crossing
6 Ueno Park
7 Tokyo National Museum
8 Tokyo Central Railway St.
9 Cosplay Go Karting
10 Tokyo Disneyland
11 Ghibli Museum
12 Gotokuji Cat Temple
13 Tokyo Imperial Palace

What to Do in Tokyo

In each chapter, we will review the top things to do in each city and region. These attractions are popular, but some will offer richer experiences during your trip.

Shinjuku Gyoen National Garden

Address: 11 Naitomachi, Shinjuku City, Tokyo 160-0014

	Garden hours	Garden gates closing time
October 1 to March 14	9 a.m. to 4 p.m.	3:30 p.m.
March 15 to June 30 and August 21 to September 30	9 a.m. to 5:30 p.m.	6 p.m.

Hours of operation: The Shinjuku Gyoen National Garden is open from Tuesday to Saturday. Additionally, as the garden is closed on Mondays, it will also be closed on Tuesdays if there is a public holiday on a Monday. It is also closed between December 29 and January 3. Everyone must be out by the time the gates close.

The Shinjuku Gyoen National Garden is one of the best ways to escape the hustle and bustle of Tokyo for a few hours. This garden dates back to the Edo era when the Naitō family lived here. It was later converted to a royal garden between 1879 and 1906.

You will find three different garden styles in this garden: Japanese traditional, landscape, and formal. Over 1,000 cherry blossom trees paint the park a stunning sea of pink in the spring, and then when autumn falls, the trees change to magnificent golds, reds, and oranges. This is also the time to visit the chrysanthemum exhibit. There is also a greenhouse with plenty of orchids, rare plants, ponds, and large trees to admire—some say it's like an indoor jungle!

Ticket type	Price
Adults	¥500
Seniors (65 and up) and students with valid ID	¥250

Senso-ji Temple

Address: 2 Chome-3-1 Asakusa, Taito City, Tokyo 111-0032

Hours of operation

- April to September: 6 a.m. to 5 p.m. daily
- October to March: 6:30 a.m. to 5 p.m. daily

Senso-ji Temple is Tokyo's oldest temple, dating back to the seventh century, and helped to shape Asakusa, a once insignificant fishing village, into a town. Given its history, this temple is one of the most visited places in Tokyo, so you can expect it to be a bit busier than other temples in the city. As you walk through the iconic Thunder Gate (Kaminarimon), you will see the famous Nakamise, a bustling street lined with traditional shops selling snacks and souvenirs. When you reach the end of the street, you'll see the Hozomon Gate leading you to the main hall of the Senso-ji Temple. The main hall is breathtaking with its impressive architecture, especially with the five-story pagoda dedicated to the Buddhist goddess of mercy, Kannon.

Various events are held at the temple annually, including Sanja Matsuri in May. However, even without the events, this is a beautiful temple to visit to get a feel for the symbolism inside.

Asakusa

The district of Asakusa became more well-known after the construction of the Senso-ji Temple. Still, this once-small fishing village is steeped in history and culture that will allow you to immerse yourself in Japan's rich heritage. Beyond Senso-ji, take the time to explore the area by exploring the Kappabashi and Shin-Nakamise Shopping Streets and the Asakusa Underground Street, Japan's oldest underground shopping centers. Additionally, you may want to take a rickshaw ride, where your guide will take you around the area and give you more history on the district. There are also water cruises along the Sumida River, providing a different view of the district. However you want to explore the district, there are many ways to do so, and it's worth spending at least half a day here if you're already planning to visit the Senso-ji Temple.

Meiji Jingu Shrine

Address: 1-1 Yoyogikamizonochō, Shibuya City, Tokyo 151-8557

Hours of operation: The shrine is open from sunrise to sunset daily.

Meiji Jingu Shrine is another excellent place to escape the hustle and bustle of Tokyo. Nestled within a dense forest adjacent to Yoyogi Park, this temple returns to the 1920s and honors Emperor Meiji and Empress Shoken. Meiji Jingu Shrine holds deep cultural and historical significance for Japan as Emperor Meiji was the first emperor of what is considered modern Japan when he ascended in the late 1860s.

As you step onto the shrine's grounds, you will be greeted by a serene atmosphere, with thousands of towering trees bringing a sense of calmness. Within the shrine, you can participate in traditional rituals, such as offering prayers in the main hall, writing wishes on wooden plaques (ema), and purifying yourself at the water basin. Additionally, the shrine sees millions of people offering prayers during the New Year.

There is no cost to visit the shrine. However, if you want to learn more about Emperor Meiji, there is the Meiji Jingu Museum on the property, which has artifacts from the shrine and some personal belongings from the emperor and empress, including a carriage that carried Emperor Meiji to the formal declaration of the Meiji Constitution. If you want to visit the museum, it is open between 10 a.m. and 4:30 p.m. from Friday to Wednesday, with the last admission at 4 p.m. Admission to the museum is ¥1,000 for adults and ¥900 for students 15 years old and under.

Beyond the shrine and the museum, a visit to the Inner Garden is also worth exploring. This is another popular spot, especially in mid-June when the irises bloom. This garden also has the Kiyomasa's Well, named after the famous samurai warrior, Kato Kyomasa. Admission to the Inner Garden is ¥500.

Tokyo Tower

Address: 4 Chome-2-8 Shibakoen, Minato City, Tokyo 105-0011

Hours of operation: 9 a.m. to 10:30 p.m. daily (last admission is at 10 p.m.)

It's often referred to as the Eiffel Tower of Tokyo, impressively standing 1,092 feet high in Central Tokyo (it's actually three meters taller than the Eiffel Tower!) This tower offers excellent views of the city, but it also has an important symbolism in Japan as it is a symbol of resilience and innovation.

Tokyo Tower was completed in 1958 in response to the country's rapid post-war economic growth and technological advancement. Its design was inspired by the Eiffel Tower (hence the nickname) and served as a broadcasting antenna in addition to Japan's emergence as a global economic power. Visitors to the tower can enjoy panoramic views of Tokyo from the main and top decks, including the

Tokyo Skytree and Mount Fuji. You can climb the 600-step staircase (or take the elevator) to get to the main deck. There are only elevators to take you to the top deck if you have a ticket for it.

The tower also has shops, restaurants, and a museum where you can learn more about its history and significance. There is also an e-sports entertainment complex called the Red Tokyo Tower, which offers various games and e-sports activities. Your ticket to the tower will allow you access to this complex for the duration of your ticket.

Ticket type	Main deck	Main deck one-day unlimited pass	Top deck tour (not available on weekends)
Adult	¥1200	¥2200	¥2800
High school student (16 to 18 years old)	¥1000	¥1800	¥2600
Student (7 to 15 years old)	¥700	¥1200	¥1800
Child (4 to 6 years old)	¥500	¥800	¥1200
Children 3 and under	Free	Free	Free

Shibuya Scramble Crossing

Shibuya Crossing is one of the most famous crossings in the world, with pedestrians crossing in all directions, which is why it has been nicknamed "scramble crossing." This pedestrian crosswalk is located outside Shibuya Station and is surrounded by towering buildings flashing neon signs. It's memorizing and chaotic to those who aren't from Tokyo (but for the locals, it's just a way to get to various points in this hub). You may need to cross the intersection at some point in your Tokyo travels, but don't feel overwhelmed by the sudden swarm of people walking in all directions from one end to the other. Know where you plan to go and embrace the vibrant atmosphere.

Ueno Park

Ueno Park is in central Tokyo, offering visitors a stunning green space to enjoy picnics, especially when the cherry blossom trees bloom. This park was established in 1873 but was once the home to the Kaneiji Temple, the wealthiest and largest temple, which belonged to the Tokugawa family during the Edo Period. Unfortunately, the temple was destroyed during the Boshin Civil War between 1868 and 1869.

In addition to the green space for you and others to enjoy, Ueno Park is home to the Tokyo National Museum and Ueno Zoo, the oldest zoo in Japan.

Tokyo National Museum

Address: 13-9 Ueno Park, Taito-ku, Tokyo, 110-8712

Hours of operation

- Sunday to Thursday: 9:30 a.m. to 5 p.m. (last admission is at 4:30 p.m.)
- Friday to Saturday: 9:30 a.m. to 7 p.m. (last admission is at 6:30 p.m.)
- Kuroda Memorial Hall: 9:30 a.m. to 5 p.m. daily
- Special exhibition hours may differ from regular operation hours.

The Tokyo National Museum, founded in 1872, is the oldest museum in Japan, and it displays an extensive collection of art and artifacts to showcase the country's rich history. This museum is situated in Ueno Park and has six buildings sprawling along the park's grounds, each big enough that they could be their own museum. As you explore the museum's vast collection of over 110,000 items, you'll see several works of art, ceramics, textiles, and archaeological artifacts. Some notable things to see include the antique Buddhist statues, scrolls, painted sliding doors, and armor worn by samurais.

Ticket type	Price
Adults	¥1000
Students 18 and under and seniors 70 and up (with valid ID)	Free

Ginza

The Ginza district is the renowned shopping area in Tokyo, dating back to the 1600s. This district offers plenty of upscale shopping boutiques, department stores, art galleries, restaurants, museums, and entertainment to explore and shop in. Even if you don't intend to shop, the vibrant atmosphere of Ginza is worth visiting to take in the architecture of some of the iconic buildings, including the Seiko House Ginza, Kabukiza Theater, and the Seiko Museum Ginza.

Tokyo Central Railway Station

Tokyo Central Railway Station is the main train hub for Tokyo, boasting stunning architecture to symbolize the city's modernization. The train station was designed and built by Kingo Tatsuno and opened to the public in 1914. Tatsuno's design was inspired by his time in England and Europe and is reflected in the iconic red-brick facade. The train station suffered some damage during World War II, but it was restored to its former glory and expanded to accommodate the growing population of Tokyo.

In addition to marveling at the stunning architecture, there are plenty of shops and restaurants you can explore inside the station. Additionally, this station will help connect you to other parts of Tokyo via subway lines, buses, and trains.

Cosplay Go Karting

Did you know you can drive a go-kart around Tokyo? If you're a fan of Mario Kart or dressing up in general, this is an unusual and fun thing to do as you drive alongside buses, cars, and trucks through Tokyo while getting to see the sights alongside a tour guide. Several companies offer this excursion, but you must have an international driver's permit. If you don't have one, you can't go karting.

Tokyo Disneyland

Address: 1-1 Maihama, Maihama, Urayasu, Chiba Prefecture 279-0031

Hours of operation: 9 a.m. to 9 p.m.

Any Disneyland you visit will be magical. However, Disneyland in Tokyo is arguably one of the better ones to see because it has food and merchandise that is exclusive to Tokyo.

It will be a busy amusement park (naturally), but you can embark on thrilling rides, including Space Mountain, Western Railroad, Pirates of the Caribbean, and the Jungle Cruise: Wildlife Expeditions.

The tickets listed in the table are a base point. However, some days may be more expensive than others.

Ticket type	Single day tickets	Weeknight passport
Adult	¥8900	¥5100
Junior	¥7400	¥5100
Child	¥5300	¥5100

Ghibli Museum

Address: 1 Chome-1-83 Shimorenjaku, Mitaka, Tokyo 181-0013

Hours of operation: From Wednesday to Monday between 10 a.m. and 6 p.m. Please note that on some Tuesdays, the museum is open, and there are some days when it will be closed outside of the regular hours of operation. When you purchase your tickets online, you can see the days when the museum is open and closed.

If you're a fan of Hayao Miyazaki's 2001 film, Spirited Away, or any of his other films, the Ghibli Museum is an enchanting destination. The director designed this museum, which resembled the world you would see in Ghibli's animated films, with its architecture, gardens, and intricate details everywhere you go. You can explore the museum's exhibits showcasing the studio's creative processes, animation techniques, and iconic characters from Spirited Away, My Neighbor Totoro, and Princess Mononoke.

There is also a theater that plays exclusive short films created by Studio Ghibli to enhance the cinematic experience. You can also browse the gift shop with plenty of Ghibli-themed merchandise and souvenirs. This is a beautiful way to immerse yourself in some of Japan's most iconic anime studios and see a different art form.

If you plan to visit the museum, you must reserve your tickets in advance, as there are no on-site sales.

Ticket type	Price
Adults (19 years old and up)	¥1000
Teens (13 to 18 years old)	¥700
Youth (7 to 12 years old)	¥400
Children (4 to 6 years old)	¥100
Children 3 and under	Free

Gotokuji Cat Temple

Address: 2 Chome-24-7 Gotokuji, Setagaya City, Tokyo 154-0021

Hours of operation: 6 a.m. to 5 p.m. daily

Gotokuji Cat Temple, also known as the Lucky Cat Temple, is a charming Buddhist temple in the Setagaya district of Tokyo. You may recognize this lucky cat symbol, or maneki-neko, as it is often in many Asian establishments. You will see this cat figurine in many Japanese restaurants and shops. However, the Gotokuji Temple is believed to be the birthplace of the symbolism of good luck and prosperity associated with the cat. When you visit this temple, you can explore the peaceful grounds adorned with hundreds of ceramic cat statues in different sizes, each with its own unique expression. If you want to bring one home, there is a temple shop where you can purchase a maneki-neko, but there is a limit of one sale per person.

Explore the Harajuku District

Harajuku district is well-known for its cosplay, unique fashion, trendy shops, and bustling atmosphere. If you explore this area, it is worth walking down Takeshita Street, a pedestrian-only lane lined with quirky boutiques, vintage shops, and trendy cafes where you can indulge in shopping for the latest fashion trends and enjoy delicious street food. It can get super busy on the weekends, but well worth it to immerse yourself in the atmosphere of the famous district.

What Events to Enjoy in Tokyo (And Around)

Events are some of the best ways to immerse yourself in Japanese culture. Attending various events in each city and region gives you a taste of what means the most to Japan and why. It's an educational and cultural experience that will help you understand a different way of living and celebrating.

Cherry Blossom Festivals

One of the most well-loved parts of Japan is its gorgeous cherry blossom trees that bloom as early as January, painting the country pink. As the spring draws nearer, the festivals to celebrate the blooming of these beautiful trees are a great way to immerse yourself in the Japanese way of celebrating spring.

During the various festivals in Tokyo, the Kanto region, and around the country, there are two-week-long celebrations that gather people in Japanese parks and gardens to see the cherry blossoms in what is called a hanami (cherry blossom viewing). These parties are outdoors and plenty of families and friends are picnicking under the trees. Some parks also have vendors who sell food and snacks.

Of the most popular spots to see the cherry blossom trees, you will want to go to Ueno Park. The Chidorigafuchi near the Imperial Palace is another great spot to visit. You can rent boats from there and ride beneath the canopy of cherry blossoms. Other places to immerse yourself in cherry blossom festivals and viewings include the Hirosaki Cherry Blossom Festival in Aomori and along the Philosopher's Path in Kyoto.

Fireworks Festivals

Fireworks festivals, known as Hanabi, occur in Tokyo and throughout Japan during summer. In Tokyo, the fireworks festival to check out is the Sumidagawa Fireworks Festival, which dates back to the 1770s. This fireworks display happens on the last Saturday of July and brings millions of spectators to watch over 20,000 fireworks launched into the night sky, taking various shapes and colors. If you want the best view of this festival, you must get there as early as possible.

Another notable fireworks festival to check out is the Tsuchiura Fireworks Competition. This event is held in late October instead of the summer months and is one of the lesser-known fireworks festivals to tourists, so you'll likely get a better vantage point to watch this innovative festival, where teams face off to create a unique display of fireworks lighting up the Tsuchiura sky.

Local Shrine Festivals

The local shrine festivals are deeply ingrained in Japanese culture and are celebrated enthusiastically with parades, vendors selling food or snacks, cultural performances, and game stalls. One of Tokyo's most popular shrine festivals is the Sanja Matsuri, which happens on the third Sunday of May (and the Friday and Saturday before it) in the Asakusa district. This shrine festival brings around 2 million people over the weekend to honor the founders of the Senso-ji Temple. Around the country, many other towns and cities host their shrine festivals. Whether you are in Tokyo or elsewhere, going to one of these is a way to get a glimpse into the unique customs and traditions surrounding these festivals.

New Year

Unlike other parts of the world, Japan welcomes the new year (shōgatsu) in its own style. This is when most families will tidy their homes, repay debts, and prepare food for the new year. Additionally, many will go to the shrines to express gratitude and pray between January 1 and 3 in a tradition known as hatsumode. If you are in Tokyo or other parts of the country over the new year, you can expect the shrines to be busier than usual, but this is also a great way to experience the new year, like those who live in Japan.

Winter Illuminations

Winter illuminations are a cherished tradition in Tokyo and around the country to brighten the streets with light displays during the dark winter months. In Tokyo, the city's central shopping districts, such as Ginza, Omotesando, and Roppongi Hills, are transformed into glittering wonderlands with elaborate light installations and festive decorations for the Christmas season. Beyond Tokyo, you can see other spectacular winter illuminations in Nagasaki, Kobe, and Osaka.

Discover the Kanto Region

The Kanto region (which translates to "east of the border") is the largest plain in Japan and has a dense population. Tokyo is one of the largest metropolises in this region. However, Yokohama is another large city in Kanto. Beyond the large cities, the region has plenty of iconic landmarks, including the Imperial Palace and Mount Fuji. Given the region's size, you'll never run out of things to see, do, and experience. However, also recognize that you won't get to do everything because of the region's size. While we have covered Tokyo and many things to do, here are a few other things to check out in the Kanto region.

What to Do in the Kanto Region

Yubatake

Yubatake is a unique and picturesque hot spring in the heart of Kusatsu. Translating to "hot water field," Yubatake has a series of wooden channels and troughs that transport mineral-rich thermal water to the surrounding ryokan and public bathhouses. Watching the water move through the troughs and onto its final destination is a mesmerizing sight. However, while you're in Kusatsu, it's worth exploring the town, especially in the evening when it's lit up.

Tokyo Imperial Palace

Address: 1-1 Chiyoda, Chiyoda City, Tokyo 100-8111

The Tokyo Imperial Palace is a historic and cultural landmark that will give you a glimpse into Japan's imperial history. The palace is on the site of the former Edo Castle, the residence of the Tokugawa shogunate during the Edo period, but is now home to the current emperor of Japan. The inner grounds are not open to the public except for guided tours and special events. However, you can explore the surrounding East Gardens, beautifully landscaped with traditional Japanese gardens and the remains of the castle's original structures, including the Nijubashi Bridge. If you opt for a tour, they take around 75 minutes, run from Tuesday to Saturday, and are on a first-come, first-served basis. The tours begin at 10 a.m. and 12:30 p.m.

Where to Eat in Tokyo and the Kanto Region

Nisshin Tasuke

Address: 4 Chome-13-18 Tsukiji, Chuo City, Tokyo 104-0045 (inside Tsukiji Outer Market)

Hours of operation: 10 a.m. to 9 p.m. daily

Tsukiji Outer Market is one of the famous spots in Tokyo where people can grab food. However, if you're looking to try unagi (freshwater eel) skewers, Nisshin Tasuke is the place to stop by in the market. Freshwater eel is one of Japan's delicacies. At this establishment, you can pick up a skewer of unagi that has been barbecued to perfection and topped with eel sauce. In addition to the unagi, Nisshin Tasuke offers other yummy skewers, including squid and clam.

Sushiro

Address: Bito Akiba Plaza, B1F 1 Chome–18–19, Sotokanda, Chiyoda , Tokyo, City, 101-0021

Hours of operation

- Monday to Friday: 11 a.m. to 11 p.m.
- Saturday and Sunday: 10:30 a.m. to 11 p.m.

Eating at a "proper" sit-down sushi establishment is excellent. But there's also something fun about eating at an establishment with sushi dishes running along a conveyor belt for patrons to grab on color-coded plates. At the end of your meal, plates will be counted to tally up your bill (every dish is around ¥120).

Harajuku Gyoza Lou

Address: 6 Chome-2-4 Jingumae, Shibuya City, Tokyo 150-0001

Hours of operation: 11:30 a.m. to 10:30 p.m. daily

Gyoza are Japanese dumplings filled with vegetables and ground meat tucked into a thin dough. While this delicious delicacy originated in China, gyoza has become a popular item in Japan and is often served with ramen, rice, or on its own. Harajuku Gyoza Lou is one of the best places to enjoy this Japanese spin on dumplings. Here, you can enjoy gyoza, either pan-fried or steamed on your own or with a side. The gyozas are made with either ground meat or ground meat, chives, and garlic (a more popular option as it has a little more flavor). This is a popular establishment, so be prepared to wait at least 30 minutes for a seat.

Oreryu Shio Ramen

Address: 150-0044 Tokyo, Shibuya City, Maruyamacho, 3–3 SSD

Hours of operation

- Monday to Saturday from 11 a.m. to 6 a.m.
- Sunday: 11 a.m. to 11 p.m.

A trip to Japan will never be complete without eating ramen at least once! Oreryu Shio Ramen is another popular Tokyo establishment serving various ramen options. One of the most unique ramen options is the butter and corn, which sounds strange, but the crunch of the corn, along with the creamy butter and salty broth, makes a delicious combination. This establishment has extended hours so that you can get your fill throughout the day and night!

Tentempura Uchitsu

Address: 5-25-4 Hiro, Shibuya-ku, Tokyo, 150-0012

Hours of operation: Monday to Saturday from 6 p.m. to 11 p.m.

Tentempura Uchitsu is a one-star Michelin restaurant and a place to escape Tokyo's hustle and bustle. This restaurant is stunning, with a massive window displaying a garden outside with bamboo, cherry blossom, and pine to splash Tentempura Uchitsu with color right when you walk in. The tempura dishes made here are created with in-season ingredients and seafood and finished with a tempura fritter. This is another intimate way to dine as you watch Chef Takahisa Uchitsu work his magic; make your reservations as soon as possible!

What to Eat in the Tokyo and the Kanto Region

Sushi

Tokyo is renowned for its fresh and expertly prepared sushi. Whether you visit a high-end sushi restaurant or a humble sushi bar, you'll find an array of sushi options, from nigiri (sliced fish over rice) to maki rolls (rolled sushi with various fillings).

Ramen

Tokyo boasts some of the best ramen shops in the world. Enjoy a steaming bowl of ramen noodles served in a rich, flavorful broth with toppings like sliced pork, soft-boiled eggs, and green onions. Each shop has its own unique style, so try different variations to find your favorite.

Tempura

Tempura is a Japanese dish of battered and deep-fried seafood and vegetables. In Tokyo, you can find tempura restaurants that serve light and crispy tempura made with fresh ingredients. Don't miss the chance to try delicate shrimp, fish, and vegetables dipped in a savory sauce.

Okonomiyaki

Okonomiyaki is a savory Japanese pancake made with a batter of flour, eggs, shredded cabbage, and various toppings like pork, shrimp, or vegetables. It's often cooked on a hot grill right at your table, allowing you to customize it to your liking with sauces and condiments.

Where to Stay in the Tokyo and the Kanto Region

Hotel Metropolitan Tokyo Ikebukuro

Address: 1 Chome-6-1 Nishiikebukuro, Toshima City, Tokyo 171-8505

If you want to stay in the Ikebukuro district, check out Hotel Metropolitan Tokyo Ikebukuro. This accommodation will connect you to several attractions, shopping centers, and public transportation. The rooms in this hotel are comfortable to ensure a relaxing stay. Some rooms also have views of the city. Prices at this hotel are about mid-range for a one-night stay.

Mitsui Garden Hotel Yokohama Minatomirai Premier

Address: 3 Chome-3-3 Minatomirai, Nishi Ward, Yokohama, Kanagawa 220-0012

The Mitsui Garden Hotel Yokohama Minatomirai Premier is a five-star option in the Kanagawa region of Kanto. It is near the Minatomirai and Takashimacho subway stations, which can take you to various parts of the area and Tokyo. The hotel has several rooms, some of which include a microwave and a washing machine. There are also two indoor swimming pools and a fitness center.

Andon Ryokan

Address: 2 Chome-34 Nihonzutsumi, Taito City, Tokyo 111-0021

Staying at any Ryokan is an experience to have at least once while you're in Japan, as it offers some of the most authentic ways to sleep and essentially live like a local. These rooms have futons to roll out and sleep on the floor. There is also a rooftop terrace and a hot tub to enjoy. If you upgrade, you can include breakfast with your room fee. Staying here is relatively cheap (around $52 per night).

First Cabin Akasaka

Address: 3 Chome-13-7 Akasaka, Minato City, Tokyo 107-0052

Capsule hotels are becoming all the rage worldwide for their compact and out-of-this-world way to rest (at least for one night). The First Cabin Akasaka is one minute from the Akasaka subway station and comes with air-conditioned units, slippers, shampoo, soap, and towels. This place does book up fast, so if you want to experience this capsule hotel, book sooner rather than later!

Park Hotel Tokyo

Address: Shiodome Media Tower 1-7-1 Higashi Shimbashi, Minato-ku 105-7227

The Park Hotel Tokyo is a luxury option for accommodations in Tokyo and boasts stunning panoramic views of the city and the Tokyo Tower from the rooms. This hotel is near several of Tokyo's attractions, including the Shiodome subway station. To enhance your stay, opt for an in-room massage to help you unwind after a day of exploring!

What Not to Do in Tokyo and the Kanto Region

Don't Miss Visiting Tokyo's Convenience Stores

Tokyo's Convinience Stores - Konbini are *actually* convenient. You'll find loads of fresh, cheap food, ATMs, copy machines, freshly ground coffee, package delivery service, and much more.

Don't Expect to Find Restaurants on the Ground Level.

In a bustling city like Tokyo, space is at a premium, leading to a unique dining setup. Many restaurants are tucked away on various building levels, not just at street level. This can be a delightful adventure, as you might find a hidden gem of a sushi bar in a basement or a cozy ramen spot on the fifth floor. It adds a sense of discovery to your dining experience, encouraging you to explore beyond the ground level and delve into the vertical expanse of Japanese urban dining.

Don't Arrive Late

If you make reservations anywhere, don't be late! One of the biggest pillars of Japanese culture is punctuality, so be mindful of your timing to ensure you arrive when you intend to. Should there be a delay on public transportation, you will be given a train delay certificate (*Densha chien shoumeisho*) to explain your tardiness.

Be Prepared to Take Your Trash Home in Tokyo

Tokyo is pretty clean for a city of its size, yet there are very few public trash cans. If you buy something from a convenience store and eat it on the spot, you can use their bins for the wrappers, and vending machines almost always have an accompanying receptacle for plastic bottles, but for the rest, you're on your own. Be prepared to take your garbage back to your hotel for disposal.

Don't Go to the Robot Restaurant

The Robot Restaurant is a popular tourist attraction but also a trap. This establishment is known for its weird show, but it's also an expensive night out. There are plenty of other great entertainment options around Tokyo that won't break the bank!

Don't Go to Golden Gai

The Golden Gai is an alley filled with bars. It's lively but really busy during the peak travel seasons if you're planning on bar hopping, and it will cost you a pretty yen just for seating charges! This is an excellent area to stop for a drink. But if you're planning a night out on the town, go to Nakano or Asakusabashi.

Dress Modestly while Visiting Senso-ji Temple

Dress modestly when visiting Senso-ji Temple. Avoid wearing revealing clothing, and consider covering tattoos if they are considered offensive in a religious context.

Follow Rituals at Senso-ji Temple

Before entering the temple's main hall, visitors are expected to purify themselves by washing their hands and mouth with water from the chozuya (water basin). Respect this tradition and participate in the purification ritual.

Don't Visit the Ghibli Museum without advance reservation.

The Ghibli Museum requires advance reservations for admission, and tickets are not sold at the door. Avoid disappointment by booking your tickets well in advance through the official website or authorized ticket vendors.

Don't disturb Resident Cats at Gotokuji Temple.

The Gotokuji Temple is famous for its association with the maneki-neko (beckoning cat) figurines, and there are many cats that roam the temple grounds. While it's tempting to interact with them, avoid chasing or disturbing the cats, as they are living creatures and deserve respect. The temple features numerous maneki-neko figurines, which are considered sacred symbols of good luck. Refrain from climbing on or touching these figurines, as they are religious artifacts and should be treated with reverence.

Don't Swim or Bathe in Yubatake

The hot spring water at Yubatake is not suitable for bathing or swimming. It's intended to view and heat nearby onsen facilities. Respect the cultural norms and avoid entering the water.

Next Stop: Mount Fuji and the Chubu Region

Tokyo is one of the most vibrant countries in Japan, with lots to see and do. In this chapter, we explored many attractions to consider checking out on your trip (including some fun ones that you may not have thought of, like cosplay go-karting!), as well as the festivals and some of the great places to eat and stay while in Tokyo and the Kanto region.

In the next chapter, we will be heading west to Mount Fuji, one of the most famous active volcanoes in the world. We'll also explore the things to do around Mount Fuji and the Chubu region.

Chapter 4:

Mount Fuji and Chubu —Dos and Don'ts

Majestic Mount Fuji is an iconic symbol of natural beauty, creating a fantastic backdrop in Japan. The volcano is active, but its last eruption was recorded in the early 1700s. While you can see Mount Fuji in the distance from various parts of Japan, including Tokyo, visiting the Chubu region is a must if you want to see this spectacular volcano up close!

Discovering the Chubu Region

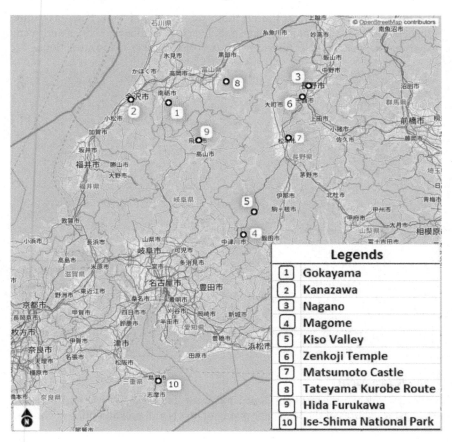

Legends	
1	Gokayama
2	Kanazawa
3	Nagano
4	Magome
5	Kiso Valley
6	Zenkoji Temple
7	Matsumoto Castle
8	Tateyama Kurobe Route
9	Hida Furukawa
10	Ise-Shima National Park

The Chubu Region, located in the central part of Japan, is one of the lesser-visited areas in the country but one of the most historically significant regions. Chubu was a vital transportation and trading hub between Japan's eastern and western parts, especially along the Nakasendo and Tokaido highways during the Edo Period. Today, it is renowned for its beautiful landscapes, including Mount Fuji and the Japanese Alps, offering hiking, skiing, and hot spring bathing opportunities. Other cultural attractions in this area include the historic villages of Shirakawa-go and Gokayama, which demonstrate some of Japan's rich heritage. Another cultural site in Chubu that should be explored is Matsumoto Castle. This region comprises nine prefectures, so you can easily spend a week exploring the area and its interesting traits. Let's get into what to do in Chubu.

What to Do in the Chubu Region

The Five Lakes Region

The Five Lakes region is on the northern side of Mount Fuji. Each lake offers excellent views of the iconic mountain and various outdoor activities and scenic experiences. Spend at least three days to explore the area's many attractions.

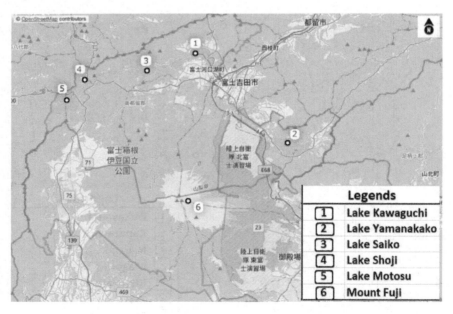

Lake Kawaguchi

Lake Kawaguchi is the most developed and accessible of the five lakes in the region. The eastern shores of the lake have plenty of hotels and ryokan options, while the west side is mostly undeveloped. While in his area, riding up the Mount Fuji Panoramic Ropeway is a must. This cable car will take you up to 1,000 meters, where you can take panoramic views of the lake and surrounding area. There are also several monuments you will see on the ride, some of which are characters from *Kachi-Kachi-Yama*, a famous Japanese folklore written by Osamu Dazai.

The Mount Fuji Panoramic Ropeway runs between 9 a.m. and 4 p.m. on weekdays (the final downhill cable car leaves at 4:20 p.m.) and from 9 a.m. to 5 p.m. on Saturdays and holidays (the final downhill cable car leaves at 5:20 p.m.). Round trips are available, or you can hike down.

Ticket type	Round trip	One way
Adult	¥1000	¥600
Child	¥500	¥150

Another great attraction to visit at Lake Kawaguchi is the Oshino Hakkai. Hakkai refers to the eight ponds surrounding the area with beautiful pathways and bridges. Visiting this small village will make you feel like you have stepped back in time, as the buildings have thatched roofs and water wheels. It also has a fantastic backdrop: Mount Fuji.

Lake Yamanakako

Lake Yamanakako is the largest lake in the Five Lakes region and less than a mile from Lake Kawaguchi. This lake is famous for outdoor enthusiasts who enjoy fishing, water sports, camping, and hiking. This lake can become quite busy in the summer due to the many sporting camps in the area for student-athletes. If you want to enjoy a hot spring, the Benifuji no Yu on the west side boasts great Mount Fuji views.

Lake Saiko

Lake Saiko offers a more secluded ambiance among its rugged shoreline, making it a favorite destination for camping and hiking. This is a great starting point for exploring hiking trails, especially the eerily gorgeous Aokigahara Forest, with trees that have grown atop lava since the ninth century. If you venture into the Aokigahara Forest, you may see rare wildlife, including the Japanese mink, wild boar, or Japanese mole. Asian black bears have also made this forest their home, so be wary if you come across one!

Another neat place to explore at Lake Saiko is the Narusawa Ice Cave. This cave is in the center of the Aokigahara Forest, and stunning frozen icicles hang from the ceiling. If you venture into this cave, remember to wear warm clothes—it is frigid!

Lake Shoji

Lake Shoji is the smallest and least developed of the five lakes, offering a serene retreat away from the crowds. This lake also borders the Aokigahara Forest and is a great place to spend some time if you want to walk along the lakeshore. This lake also boasts some of the best views of Mount Fuji.

Lake Motosu

Lake Motosu is renowned for its crystal-clear waters and postcard-perfect views of Mount Fuji from the northeastern side, making it a favorite spot for photography enthusiasts and nature lovers. At this lake, you can rent kayaks to explore the lake's pristine waters or enjoy the landscape by relaxing along the lakeshore. If you are there in the spring between April and May, you'll see plenty of flowers blooming to add a touch of color to the area.

Shirakawa-Go and Gokayama

The villages of Shirakawa-Go and Gokayama are two UNESCO World Heritage Sites famous for their picturesque scenery and traditional gassho-zukuri farmhouses characterized by their steeply thatched roofs to withstand heavy snowfall. Some people feel like they have entered a fairytale when they visit these two villages, especially in the winter when the houses are covered with snow. When you visit these villages, you can immerse yourself in the timeless charm of rural Japan while exploring these well-preserved communities.

While you're here, it's also worth exploring the quaint streets of Ogimachi Village, the largest village in Shirakawa-Go. You'll also want to make sure you visit Wada-Ke House, the former house of one of the wealthiest families in the town, which is now a museum. It is open 9 a.m. to 5 p.m. daily. Admission is ¥400 for adults and ¥250 for children.

For other scenic explorations, check out the beautiful hamlets of Ainokura and Suganuma Village in Gokayama. Ainokura is the largest farmhouse area in Gokoyama and also the most rural. Many still live here, but it is worth strolling along the beautiful streets and taking in the farmlands. On the other hand, Suganuma is the smallest farming town in Gokayama. While here, be sure to go to the Folk Museum, where you can see everyday items and tools used for farming. The Folk Museum is open daily from 9 a.m. to 4:30 p.m. except from December to March, when it closes at 4 p.m., Admission is ¥300 for adults and ¥150 for children.

Kanazawa

Kanazawa is a famous and well-preserved village dating back to the Edo period. It was the home of the Maeda Clan, the second most powerful family to follow Tokugawa. Because of this family, the village earned many agricultural achievements due to its rice production.

Beyond its accolades, Kanazawa has a rich samurai heritage, which can be explored in the Nagamachi Samurai District. At this well-preserved site, you'll see samurai residences lining the streets. To get a more in-depth look at the samurai lifestyle, you can go to Nomura-ke. This former samurai residence has artifacts on display depicting the thriving life of being a samurai. This museum is located at 1-3-32 Naga-machi, Kanazawa, Ishikawa, and their operating hours are 8:30 a.m. to 5:30 p.m. daily between April and September and from 8:30 a.m. to 4:30 p.m. between October and March.

Another famous area in Kanazawa is the Kenrokuen Garden, one of Japan's most beautiful gardens featuring scenic ponds, seasonal flora, and well-maintained landscaped hills. This is a pretty garden to stroll through no matter what time of the year, but visiting during the spring when the cherry blossoms bloom, and the autumn when the trees turn orange, gold, and red will make for some stunning photos.

If you want to check out a temple, the Ninjadera Temple is worth visiting. This temple has many traps and secret doors, which made it an essential building for secret attacks to defend against intruders. This temple can be visited on guided tours only. Tours are held between 9 a.m. and 4 p.m. and run every 30 to 60 minutes. Please note that infants are not allowed into the temple if you are traveling with them.

One final place you should explore in Kanazawa is the historic Higashi Chaya District. This was once a geisha district back in the Edo period. Chances are you won't see a real geisha, but you will see the old buildings that have since been repurposed into tea houses and gift shops.

Ticket type	Nomura-ke	Ninjadera Temple
Adult	¥550	¥1200
Children	¥400	¥800

Nagano

Nagano is located in the Japanese Alps and is home to the famous Zenkoji Temple, one of Japan's most worshiped Buddhist sites. You can explore centuries-old religious traditions and architecture in this historic town in the city's historic districts.

Tsumago-Juku and Magome

Nakasendo is one of the roads worth exploring to taste Nagano's rich history. This was the longest of the five roads connecting Japan to Edo, covering 334 miles and going through 69 post-towns. Of those famous post-towns to explore is Tsumago-juku, which has several wooden buildings. This town hasn't changed, and you'll see the roofs of inns still weighed down by heavy stones. In the evening, the street is lit by paper lanterns, making you feel like you've stepped back in time.

As you continue to follow Nakasendo, you'll eventually end up in the village of Magome. This village has beautiful buildings from the Edo era lining stone-paved streets. This town is slightly more developed than Tsumago, with more shops and restaurants. It also boasts gorgeous views of Mount Etna.

This hike should take up to three hours, depending on your fitness level. However, the terrain is rugged at times. If you have luggage you want to transfer between the two post-towns, baggage delivery is offered between late March and the end of November. This service is ¥1000 per bag.

Kiso Valley

For another outdoor hiking excursion, check out the Kiso Valley trail, which runs alongside the center of the Japanese Alps. This 43-mile trail once served as a trade route. It will also bring you to Tsumago-Juku, Magome, and Narai, which boast charming historical buildings that have not changed much in their years.

Zenkoji Temple

Address: 491-I, Oaza Nagano Motozen-cho, Nagano City, Nagano Prefecture 380-0851

Hours of operation: The temple is open one hour before sunrise until 4:30 p.m. daily, except December to February when it closes at 4 p.m., and March and November when it closes at 4 p.m. The museum is open from 9 a.m. to 4 p.m. daily all year.

Zenkoji Temple dates back to the seventh century and houses Japan's first Buddhist statue, which is interestingly hidden. A copy of this statue is only revealed to the public every six years. Depending on when you are planning your trip, there is much to discover in this historic temple, given that it has played a significant role in helping shape Nagano.

At this temple, you can explore the inner chamber of the main altar. If you are brave, you can go to the basement and walk through a blackened passageway to search for the "key to paradise." Legend has it that those who find the key attached to a wall will be given redemption.

After exploring the temple, I found the museum behind the main hall worth exploring. You can see a collection of different Buddhas and Bodhisattvas on display here.

There is an admission fee to visit the inner part of the temple (Naijin of the Hondo), take the O-Kaidan Tour, or visit the museum. Tickets can be purchased from a machine on the right side of the main entrance. Otherwise, entrance to the temple precincts and outer sanctuary is free.

Ticket type	Price
Adults	¥600
Students (Grades 10 to 12)	¥200
Students (Grades 1 to 9)	¥50
Preschool-aged children	Free

Matsumoto Castle

Address: 4-1 Marunouchi, Matsumoto, Nagano 390-0873

Hours of operation

- 8:30 a.m. to 5 p.m. daily (the last entry is at 4:30 p.m.)

- If you are in Japan over the summer, the hours are extended to 6 p.m., and the last admission time is 5:30 p.m.

Matsumoto Castle is one of Japan's most iconic and well-preserved historical landmarks, dating back to the 1590s. It is situated in Nagano and is famous for its black exterior. It is built on plains rather than a mountain or hillside. Inside the castle, you'll explore its unique interior and take in beautiful views of the Japanese Alps and surrounding area from the observation deck on the top floor. This area is popular in the springtime when the cherry blossoms are blooming.

Ticket type	Price
Adults	¥700
Children (6 to 15 years old)	¥300
Children 5 and under	Free

Tateyama Kurobe Alpine Route

The Tateyama Kurobe Alpine Route is a beautiful journey through the Northern Japanese Alps. It offers stunning mountain landscapes, dramatic towering peaks, deep gorges, and pristine alpine lakes between Nagano, Toyama, and Omachi Town. The route is open between mid-April and November 30.

There are several ways to follow the Tateyama Kurobe Alpine Route via ropeway, cable cars, highland, and trolley buses, walking the snow corridor, and taking the Toyama Chiho Railway, which will give different perspectives of the alpine scenery. You can follow several observation points and other hiking trails, especially at Murodo, where you'll get fantastic views of the Tateyama Mountain Range. If you are taking the Tateyama Trolley, there is a transfer point with an observation deck that offers excellent mountain views. To view the towering snow walls along the snow corridor, you will want to follow the road that runs between Bijodaira and Murodo. Between April and mid-June, the road is open to pedestrian-only traffic for viewing these impressive walls.

Hida Furukawa

Hida Furukawa is a small town in the Gifu Prefecture famous for its timber, the craftsmanship of the carpenters, and well-preserved buildings. In this town, you can meander along the quaint streets, admiring the architecture and the Seto River, which runs through Hida Furukawa. This town is also known for its annual festivals, including the Furukawa Festival, which takes place every April and features a display of parade floats (which you can see at the Festival Hall if you're in Japan at a different point in the year).

Ise-Shima National Park

Ise-Shima National Park is a stunning coastal paradise in the Mie Prefecture. This national park spans over 137,000 acres of diverse range landscapes, from rugged coastlines and beautiful beaches to dense forests and scenic islands, offering plenty of outdoor activities to enjoy and cultural experiences. One of the park's most iconic attractions is the Ise Jingu, an ancient shrine dating back 2,000 years dedicated to the mythical Amaterasu Omikami. If you want to learn more about the shrine, the park offers guided tours that will give you a more in-depth history of the architectural styles used.

The park has plenty of observation areas to take in the different sights. They are the Yokoyama Observatory, which gives panoramic views of Ago Bay; Mount Asama Observatory, which provides panoramic views of the Shima, Atsumi, and Chita Peninsulas; and the Nankai Observatory, which shows the beautiful Gokasho Bay.

Beyond the observatories and the shrine, Ise-Shima National Park offers plenty of outdoor experiences, including kayaking, hiking, and wildlife watching. This national park also boasts plenty of seafood, which you can enjoy at one of the many local eateries.

Climbing Mount Fuji

Climbing Mount Fuji is an exciting experience. It is best done between early July and September when the weather is most favorable. However, even though there are trails to follow, it requires careful planning and preparation, especially if you plan to start at the bottom and hike to the top instead of taking the bus halfway.

While climbing Mount Fuji, ensure you have sturdy hiking shoes and bring plenty of water, snacks, and sunscreen. It's also essential to have clothing that can protect you from various weather elements, as you can still face challenging weather conditions and strong winds. Additionally, as you will be climbing a higher altitude, it's possible to feel sick. You can pick up an oxygen canister to prevent it at a station or mountain hut.

There are several trails to choose from, with the Yoshida Trail being the most popular and well-maintained route. Along the Yoshida Trail, you will encounter mountain huts with restrooms, food, and shelter, but it is advisable to bring cash as credit cards may not be accepted. It should take about six hours for the ascent and another four hours for the descent. If you take the Yoshida Trail, it's best to plan for an overnight to break the hike up into two parts. Accommodations are available around the seventh and eighth stations. Other paths you can take include

- the Fujinomiya Trail, a steeper and more challenging hike.
- the Subashiri Trail, which is less crowded but also doesn't have as many mountain huts with amenities.
- the Gotemba Trail is the longest hiking trail you can follow.
- the Ohachi-Meguri Trail, which is a hike around the crater that will give you full views of Japan.

What Events to Enjoy in the Chubu Region

Gifu Nobunaga Festival

The Gifu Nobunaga Festival is an annual event held in Gifu to commemorate the legacy of Oda Nobunaga, one of Japan's most influential historical figures. For a quick history of who Nobunaga was, he was a powerful feudal lord in Japan during the 16th century who played a pivotal role in unifying half of Japan during the tumultuous Sengoku period. Nobunaga was known for his strategic brilliance, innovative military tactics, and ruthless determination to centralize power under his rule. He effectively used firearms, introduced battlefield tactics, and implemented administrative reforms to strengthen his authority as a Japanese warrior and government official. Furthermore, Nobunaga was known for supporting foreign trade and fostering cultural development, ending toll roads, which the local daimyo had been privileged to receive as a source of income. Despite Nobunaga's significant accomplishments, his life was cut short when one of his generals, Akechi Mitsuhide, betrayed him in June 1582.

The festival to celebrate Nobunaga takes place on the first Saturday and Sunday of November. During this festival, you can immerse yourself in this rich cultural celebration and see people dressed up like Nobunaga's generals, Saito Dosun, and his calvary to pay homage to Nobunaga's reign. Additionally, marching bands parade through the streets of Gifu, and there are food vendors and much more to see and experience. This is an exciting event and not one to miss if you are in Japan in November!

Where to Eat in the Chubu Region

Wappameshi Inakaya

Address: 9-1457 Furumachidori, Chuo-ku, Niigata City, Niigata 951-8063
Hours of operation: 11:30 a.m. to 2:30 p.m. and 5 p.m. to 9 p.m. daily

Wappameshi Inakaya is a mid-range establishment offering seasonal seafood dishes and other specialties alongside *wappa meshi*, steamed rice in a wooden box with your choice of toppings. This restaurant also has course options with seven dishes you can enjoy, which are relatively inexpensive, especially if you split them with others. Many visitors to this restaurant are big fans of the grilled flounder (*yanagi karei hitohoshi-yaki*) and the sashimi choices.

Kastanie Karuizawa Roast Chicken

Address: 23-2 Karuizawa Higashi, Nagano-ken 389-0104
Hours of operation: Thursday to Monday between 4 p.m. and 9 p.m.

Kastanie Karuizawa Roast Chicken is an excellent place to eat if you're craving European food. This establishment specializes in rotisserie chicken, served alongside other healthy dishes and salads with local produce. They also have a great wine and beer selection and Japanese sodas. Prices at Kastanie Karuizawa Roast Chicken are about mid-range.

Legian

Address: 2-31-30 Katamachi Social Lejac Bldg. 1F, Kanazawa, Ishikawa Prefecture 920-0981
Hours of operation

- Monday to Friday: 5 p.m. to 11 p.m.
- Saturday and Sunday: 5 p.m. to 2 a.m.

At Legian, you'll find a blend of different cuisines as the cooks at this establishment bring together Indonesian and Japanese flavors, creating a delicious fusion of the two cuisine types. This establishment is pretty cheap, and you can expect plenty of Japanese dishes that incorporate Indonesian spices.

Also, if you're looking for a nightlife experience, Legian has a bar called Pole Pole, open from 11 p.m. to 5 a.m.

Kakusho

Address: 2-98 Babacho-dori, Takayama, Gifu-ken 506-0838
Hours of operation: 11:30 a.m. to 3 p.m. and 5:30 p.m. to 10 p.m. daily

Kakusho is set in a beautiful Edo-period house with lovely garden views. However, its famous vegetarian temple food (*shojin ryori*) brings people here to eat. This restaurant has a menu that is constantly changing based on the season. In addition to vegetarian options, they also have fish, tempura, and soba noodles. This is a bit of a fancier night out, but it is worth it as the owner often speaks with the patrons to explain the dishes.

Fujiya Gohonjin

Address: 80 Daimon-cho, Nagano, Nagano-ken 380-0841
Hours of operation

- Sunday to Thursday: 11 a.m. to 3 p.m. and 5:30 p.m. to 9:30 p.m.
- Friday: 11 a.m. to 3 p.m. and 5:30 p.m. to 10 p.m.
- Saturday: 7 p.m. to 10 p.m.

In a stunning building, Fujiya Gohonjin is a restaurant offering Italian cuisine made with fresh, locally sourced ingredients. You can choose the course option for lunch or dinner, which comes with a set number of dishes made with different flavors. Additionally, there is a dinner a la carte option if you don't want a full-course meal. If you plan to eat here, you will want to book a reservation, which can be made through their website.

What to Eat in the Chubu Region

Hida Beef

Hida Beef is a premium wagyu beef that originates from the Hida region in Gifu Prefecture. Known for its exceptional marbling and tenderness, Hida Beef is often served as steak or in hotpot dishes like sukiyaki and shabu-shabu. Don't miss the chance to savor this melt-in-your-mouth delicacy.

Takayama Ramen

Takayama Ramen is a regional specialty of Takayama City in Gifu Prefecture. Unlike the rich and heavy tonkotsu ramen found in other regions, Takayama Ramen features a clear and light soy sauce-based broth, topped with sliced pork, green onions, and bamboo shoots. It's a comforting and flavorful dish that showcases the local flavors of the region.

Toyama Black Ramen

Toyama Black Ramen, also known as Kuro Ramen, hails from Toyama Prefecture. This unique ramen features a jet-black broth made from soy sauce, miso, and roasted garlic, giving it a rich and complex flavor. Topped with slices of pork, green onions, and a seasoned soft-boiled egg, Toyama Black Ramen is a must-try for ramen enthusiasts.

Miso Katsu

Miso Katsu is a beloved dish in Nagoya, Aichi Prefecture. It features a breaded and deep-fried pork cutlet (tonkatsu) served with a rich and savory miso-based sauce. The combination of crispy fried pork and umami-rich miso sauce creates a satisfying and flavorful meal. Miso Katsu is often accompanied by shredded cabbage and rice, making it a hearty and comforting dish.

Hoba Miso

Hoba Miso is a traditional dish from the Gifu Prefecture, particularly the Hida region. It consists of miso paste, tofu, mushrooms, and vegetables grilled on a magnolia leaf (hoba) over an open flame. The magnolia leaf imparts a subtle aroma to the dish, enhancing its flavor. Hoba Miso is a delicious and hearty dish that captures the essence of rural Japanese cuisine.

Where to Stay in the Chubu Region

Yatsusankan

Address: 1 Chome-8-27 Furukawacho Mukaimachi, Hida, Gifu 509-4241
Yatsusankan is a ryokan that blends traditional Japanese hospitality with modern comfort. This establishment's various rooms are tatami-mat designed, complete with shoji screens and minimalist décor. This accommodation is about six minutes from the Japan Rail Hida-Furukawa Train Station, has family-sized rooms, and has a hot spring bath. It also offers massages.

Hotel Nikko Niigata

Address: 5-1 Bandaijima, Chuo Ward, Niigata 950-0078
This accommodation will not break your budget for a four-star hotel, even if you stay here for a weekend! The Hotel Nikko Niigata is a stunning hotel with rooms that overlook the Japan Sea and the Northern Japanese Alps. All rooms are fitted with massive windows to let in plenty of daylight. The rooms also have a fridge, a kettle, and tea bags. There is also a restaurant on-site that offers breakfast at an additional cost.

Toyoko Inn Niigata Furumachi

Address: 7 Bancho-1168-2 Kamiokawamaedori, Chuo Ward, Niigata, 951-8068
Located just outside the city center of Niigata, Toyoko Inn Niigata Furumachi is a three-star hotel that offers comfort and convenience without breaking your budget. The rooms have modern amenities to ensure comfort, and some have sea views. Additionally, a buffet breakfast is included with your room fee.

Ryokan Biyunoyado

Address: 2951-1 Hirao, Yamanochi, Shimotakai District, Nagano 381-0401
Ryokan Biyunoyado offers traditional Japanese accommodations with a focus on relaxation and rejuvenation. If you stay at this ryokan, you can stay in a traditional

Japanese-style room with woven straw mats and a futon or a Western-style bed. Ryokan Biyunoyado also has indoor and outdoor hot spring baths you can take advantage of; there is also a private hot spring bath you can book, but you will be charged an additional fee.

Matsumoto Hotel Kagetsu

Address: 4 Chome-8-9 Ote, Matsumoto, Nagano 390-0874

Matsumoto Hotel Kagetsu has been around since 1887, making it the oldest accommodation in the area. Its prime location puts you steps away from Matsumoto Castle, making it an ideal base to explore the landmarks in Nagano. This hotel also offers massage services.

What Not to Do in the Chubu Region

Don't Expect Spring Temperatures

Don't expect mild temperatures when visiting Mount Fuji in the springtime. Pack clothing that can keep you warm and dry, as it can be pretty rainy in these areas.

Beware of Altitude Sickness at Mount Fuji

The human body requires some time to adjust to a sudden increase in altitude. Otherwise, there is a risk of headache, dizziness, and nausea. Quite a few people who climb Mount Fuji suffer from altitude sickness. To avoid altitude sickness, you are advised to tackle the mountain slowly, stay hydrated, and take frequent breaks. An overnight stay at a hut around the 7th or 8th station is recommended instead of a straight climb to the top. Small bottles of oxygen, available at the 5th station and mountain huts, can effectively prevent and fight altitude sickness; however, the only reliable treatment is to descend the mountain.

Don't Touch or Lean on the Walls at Matsumoto Castle

As Matsumoto Castle is centuries old, avoid touching or leaning on the walls to preserve its characteristics and integrity. Also, avoid climbing in prohibited areas that can damage the structure or pose safety risks.

Don't Skip having a Meal at Hida Furukawa.

Hida Furukawa is known for its delicious Hida beef, local sake, and traditional crafts such as Hida Shunkei lacquerware. During your visit, don't miss the opportunity to sample these regional specialties and support local businesses.

Check the Weather Forecast before embarking on the Tateyama Kurobe Route.

The Tateyama Kurobe Alpine Route is subject to rapidly changing weather conditions, including snowfall and avalanches, especially during the winter months. Check the weather forecast and road conditions before embarking on the route, and heed any warnings or advisories issued by local authorities. The Alpine Route passes through pristine natural landscapes, including mountain forests, alpine meadows, and glacier-fed lakes. Avoid littering, picking plants, or disturbing wildlife to preserve the beauty and ecological integrity of these environments. The Tateyama Kurobe Alpine Route offers breathtaking scenery and unique cultural attractions, such as the Snow Corridor and Kurobe Dam. Take your time to savor the experience, snap photos, and immerse yourself in the beauty of Japan's Northern Alps.

Show Respect to Natives while visiting Shirakawa-Go and Gokayama.

Shirakawa-Go and Gokayama are UNESCO World Heritage Sites known for their traditional Gassho-style houses and rural landscapes. Show respect for local customs, traditions, and cultural heritage by following any posted rules or guidelines and refraining from disruptive behavior. Many of the Gassho-style houses in Shirakawa-Go and Gokayama are still inhabited by local residents. Avoid climbing on or entering private property without permission to respect the privacy of residents and preserve the integrity of the historic buildings.

Swimming is not safe in Five Lake Regions.

Most of the lakes in the Five Lake Region are not suitable for swimming due to their depth, currents, and lack of designated swimming areas. Avoid entering the water to prevent accidents or injuries.

Next Stop: Kyoto and the Kansai Region

The Chubu region is a great off-the-beaten-path excursion for outdoor activities, historical sites, and marvels at the grand Mount Fuji. This chapter has given you a comprehensive guide on what you can do and enjoy in this central part of Japan to fully immerse yourself in this beautiful region's stunning landscape and landmarks. In the next chapter, we will venture west to the Kansai region and Kyoto, where plenty of ancient secrets exist to learn and discover.

Chapter 5:

Kyoto and Kansai Region — Dos and Don'ts

O f all the places to see various temples and shrines in Japan, Kyoto is the best place to do so. The city has an impressive 3,000 temples and shrines, so it has been nicknamed "The City of 10,000 Shrines." But there is so much more about Kyoto that makes this ancient city exceptional!

Discovering Kyoto

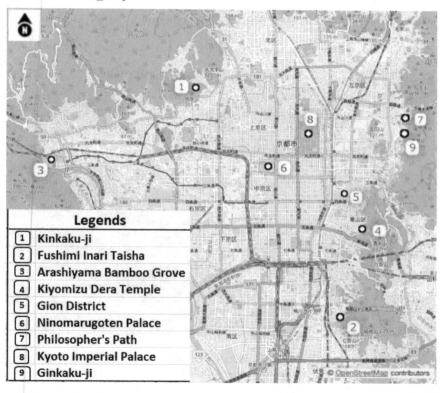

Legends	
1	Kinkaku-ji
2	Fushimi Inari Taisha
3	Arashiyama Bamboo Grove
4	Kiyomizu Dera Temple
5	Gion District
6	Ninomarugoten Palace
7	Philosopher's Path
8	Kyoto Imperial Palace
9	Ginkaku-ji

Kyoto, once the capital of Japan until 1868, has a rich heritage dating back over 1,000 years, making it the heart of traditional Japanese culture. Kyoto is renowned for its numerous UNESCO World Heritage sites, including the Kinkaku-ji (Golden

Pavilion), the Kiyomizu-Dera Temple, and the To-ji Temple. However, the towering mountains surrounding the city also add a beautiful backdrop to this ancient city.

Kyoto's cultural attractions extend beyond its UNESCO World Heritage sites. This city has been well-preserved compared to other parts of Japan, where devastating earthquakes and fires have impacted the buildings. Kyoto also works to hold onto its ancient traditions, passing them down between generations. Many shops have been around for years; some still sell handmade paper (*washi*) and tea canisters (*chazutsu*).

What to Do in Kyoto

Kinkaku-ji

Address: 1 Kinkakujicho, Kita Ward, Kyoto 603-8361

Hours of operation: 9 a.m. to 5 p.m. daily

Kinkaku-ji, also known as the Golden Pavilion, is a Zen Buddhist temple and UNESCO World Heritage site renowned for its stunning gold-leaf-covered exterior that shimmers in the sun. Kinkaku-ji's history dates back to the Kamakura period (between 1185 and 1333) when aristocrat Saionji Kintsune lived in a villa. It eventually caught the eye of Ashikaga Yoshimitsu, a powerful shogun, who bought the land and built his villa in 1397. When he died, the villa was converted into a Zen Buddhist temple.

Of course, the main highlight of visiting Kinkaku-ji is the impressive golden exterior shine and the reflections cast in the surrounding pond. While you can't go inside the temple, you can explore the surrounding temple grounds and take in the serene beauty of the temple from various viewpoints around the pond. Additionally, you can explore the former living quarters of the head priest to see the painted sliding doors and enjoy tea in their small tea garden. Admission to the temple grounds is ¥500 per person, and it's best to go earlier in the day as it can get quite busy in the afternoon.

Fushimi Inari Taisha

Address: 68 Fukakusa Yabunouchicho, Fushimi Ward, Kyoto 612-0882

Fushimi Inari Taisha is a well-known shrine founded in 711 by the Hata family as a dedication to Inari, the Shinto deity of rice. While one of the primary reasons visitors make their way to this shrine is to explore the surrounding trails of Mount Inari, many people come to marvel and walk through the shrine vermilion (orange-colored) torii gates, which form winding paths through the forest. In addition to exploring the paths and trails, you will also have the opportunity to explore the main hall and stone fox statues, which are believed to be the messengers of Inari. If you plan to hike to the summit of Mount Inari, it should take up to three hours, depending on your fitness level.

Arashiyama Bamboo Grove

Address: Near the Tenryu-ji Temple (68 Susukinobaba-cho, Saga-Tenryuji, Ukyo-ku, Kyoto Prefecture)

Arashiyama Bamboo Grove feels like you are stepping into an enchanted forest with its towering bamboo stalks lining a winding pathway. It is unlike any other forest you have ever ventured through. Although it is a short walk, it is a nice break from the hustle and bustle of Kyoto as the swaying sounds of the bamboo stalks and their leaves rustling in the breeze create a soothing sound that enhances the peaceful ambiance.

As you walk the path, it will bring you to Okochi-Sanso Villa, the former villa of Japanese actor Denjirō Ōkōchi. To go inside and explore the gardens will cost ¥1000, but you'll get to admire the traditional Japanese architecture from the inside out. This admission will also give you access to a tea house where you can enjoy a cup of matcha tea and a sweet. This villa is open from 9 a.m. to 5 p.m., and its address is 8 Sagaogurayama Tabuchiyamacho, Ukyo Ward, Kyoto, 616-8394.

Of course, Arashiyama Bamboo Grove is also a great place to take photos for Instagram, so make sure your phone and camera are charged!

Kiyomizu-Dera Temple

Address: 1 Chome-294 Kiyomizu, Higashiyama Ward, Kyoto, 605-0862

Hours of operation: 6 a.m. to 6 p.m. daily (hours are subject to change based on season)

Kiyomizu-dera Temple is one of the most famous and popular temples in Kyoto. Its main temple hall's veranda is built out of the side of Mount Otowa. It's an impressive site with plenty of history attached to it. The wooden veranda you see today dates back to 1633; however, when the temple was initially built and founded in the eighth century, its stage was the setting for traditional Japanese performances dedicated to the Buddhist deity, Kannon.

As you explore the temple grounds, you will see other temple halls, pagodas, and the Jishu-jinja Shrine, famous for its matchmaking stones. Legend says you will find your partner if you can walk across them with your eyes closed.

Whatever brings you to this temple, there is plenty to see, do, and enjoy within these sacred temple grounds.

Ticket type	Price
Adults	¥500
Junior high and elementary school students	¥200

Gion District

At one point, Gion District, situated along the Kamo River, was a resting place for pilgrims to the Yasaka Shrine (formerly Gion Shrine). Today, it is a renowned part of Kyoto that is famous for preserving its former geisha life. This is one of the districts you should visit without an agenda. Stroll along the narrow streets and admire the traditional *machiya* houses, many of which have been converted to art galleries and sellers, antique shops, kimono stores, and other craft shops. Of course, as geishas often frequented teahouses, there are many you can stop into throughout the district. However, the most famous and oldest teahouse is Ichiriki Ochaya. This teahouse has been around for three centuries, and at one point, it was the residence of the revolutionary samurai warriors 47 Ronin.

While wandering through Gion, you may see a geisha or maiko (apprentice geisha) in their distinctive attire as they move between engagements. You can also catch their performances at the Hanami-koji Theater. Some other places to explore in Gion are the famous Tatsumi Bridge that connects the banks of the Shirakawa Canal, Shinbashi Dori, where you can see glowing lanterns in the evening, and the Yasaka Shrine.

Nijō-jō and Ninomaru-Goten Palace

Address: 541 Nijo Jocho, Horikawa Nishiiri, Nakagyo-ku, Kyoto 604-8301

Hours of operation: 8:45 a.m. to 5 p.m. daily (closed between December 29 and 31)

Nijō-jō Castle is a UNESCO World Heritage site and a place where you can get a glimpse into Japan's feudal past. This fortress's construction began in 1601, commissioned by the founder of the Tokugawa shogunate, Tokugawa Ieyasu. However, as Ieyasu was in his sixties by the time construction began, he didn't see the castle when it was finished in 1626. When the castle was completed, it became the place for the Tokugawa shogunate to stay when they made official visits to Kyoto.

The castle is famous for its elaborate architectural design, featuring extensive stone walls, moats, and two concentric rings of fortifications. Within the castle grounds are several other buildings and gardens to explore, including the Ninomaru Palace, where you can admire historical artwork in the painting gallery on movable panels and walk the *ugishubari* (nightingale floors) corridor, which squeaks. At the time, this purpose was to alert the shogunate of intruders. Additionally, the Seiryu-ēn Garden offers a tranquil retreat with beautiful ponds and two teahouses where you can immerse yourself in traditional Japanese tea ceremonies.

Ticket type	Nijō-jō Castle	Nijō-jō Castle and Ninomaru Palace	Painting Gallery
Adults	¥800	¥1300	¥100
Junior high/high school students	Free	¥400	¥100
Primary school students	Free	¥300	¥100

Philosopher's Path

The Philosopher's Path is a scenic walking trail along the Shishigatani Canal. This beautiful and tranquil path was named after the famous Japanese philosopher Kitarō Nishida, who was known to walk this path as a way of practicing moving meditation as he walked to work at Kyoto University.

The Philosopher's Path is worth visiting during cherry blossom season, as it is lined with many cherry blossom trees that paint the scenery pink with their blossoms. This path is also great to walk when autumn comes in, and the foliage changes to bright red, orange, and gold. This path also passes by several temples and shrines, including the Hōnen-in, with a stunning moss-covered gate and a stone bridge to admire, and the Ōtoyo-jinja shrine, where mice statues guard the entrance.

The best way to the Philosopher's Path is to take the 5 or 17 bus from Kyoto Station and get off at Ginkakuji-michi.

Kyoto Imperial Palace

Address: 3 Kyōtogyoen, Kamigyo Ward, Kyoto 602-0881

Hours of operation: 9 a.m. to 4 p.m. (closed on Monday and Tuesday)

The Kyoto Imperial Palace served as the residence of the Imperial Family from 1331 until 1869, when the capital was moved to Tokyo. It was initially built in 794 as the Heian-kyō Palace (which means capital of peace). Kyoto Imperial Palace has been rebuilt several times over the centuries due to fires or being struck by lightning. Each time it burned down, it was rebuilt in the same spot—though, over time, the Imperial Family stopped rebuilding the structure following several lightning strikes and fires.

The existing structure at the Kyoto Imperial Palace dates back to the 19th century when the Tokugawa shogunate restored it to preserve the original palace's architectural style.

When you visit Kyoto Imperial Palace, you can explore the gardens and expansive grounds surrounding the palace. If you want to see the inside of the palace, you must take a guided tour for free. The English-guided tours are at 10 a.m. and 2 p.m. and are about 50 minutes long.

Ginkaku-Ji

Address: 2 Ginkakujichō, Sakyo Ward, Kyoto 606-8402

Hours of operation

- March to November: 8 a.m. to 5 p.m.
- December to February: 9 a.m. to 4:30 p.m.

Ginkaku-Ji, also known as the Silver Pavilion, is a Zen Buddhist temple dating back to 1482. This beautiful temple is along the eastern mountains of Higashiyama. It has an interesting background on why it was called the Silver Temple, even though it is not adorned in silver like its counterpart, the Kinkaku-ji. The temple was initially built as a retirement villa by Ashikaga Yoshimasa, the eighth Muromachi shogunate leader, modeled after the Kinkaku-ji. As for the nickname Silver

Pavilion, some believe the temple got its name to differentiate it from Kinkaku-ji. Others say it is because the pavilion glows silver when the moon's light reflects on the exterior of the building. The villa was converted to a Zen temple when Yoshimasa died in 1490.

As you visit the grounds of Ginkaku-Ji, you can follow the circular route through the temple's moss and sand gardens. Six other temple buildings are throughout the property, but you won't be able to enter any of them, including the Ginkaku-Ji.

What Events to Enjoy in Kyoto

Hanatoro

Hanatoro, which translates to "flower and light road," is an annual event held in Kyoto in March (in the Higashiyama district) and December (in the Arashiyama district). During this event, streets are adorned with thousands of lanterns, creating a beautiful glowing pathway to explore. If you are in Kyoto during this 10-day event, you will get to take in the lovely atmosphere while taking in the sights of the shrines and temples in Kyoto and stopping in the shops that have extended their hours. Additionally, various cultural performances occur during the event, allowing you to immerse yourself in Japanese culture. This is one of the most magical events, so check out if you will be in Kyoto in March or December!

Jidai Matsuri (Festival of Ages)

Jidai Matsuri, also known as the Festival of Ages, is an annual parade in Kyoto on October 22. This event features a colorful procession of participants dressed in period costumes to represent various eras of Japanese history, spanning from the Meiji period to the Enryaku period. The participants in this 2.5-hour parade walk from the Imperial Palace to the Heian Shrine, and you will see all sorts of people represented, including warriors, priests, merchants, and commoners, walking the stretch between these iconic landmarks.

Kobo-ichi Market

Address: 1 Kujocho, Minami Ward, Kyoto 601-8473

The Kobo-ichi Market in Kyoto is held on the 21st of every month at the To-ji Temple, commemorating the death of the monk Kukai. You will find various goods at this market, including bargain souvenirs, clothing, and food. Apart from shopping, the flea market provides an opportunity to experience other beautiful Japanese architecture on the temple grounds. To-ji Temple is a UNESCO World Heritage site famous for its towering pagoda, which holds the record as the tallest wooden building in the country. Additionally, you can explore Kukai's house, the Miedo Building.

Discovering the Kansai Region

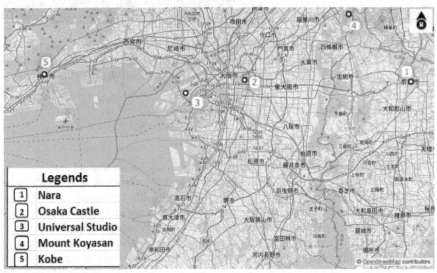

Given that Kyoto is the heart of traditional Japanese culture, it should come as no surprise that the Kansai Region also has plenty of historical significance as it served as Japan's political and cultural center for many years. In the general region, there are many areas to explore, including Nara, which was the first capital of Japan before Kyoto; Osaka, which is Japan's third largest city; Wakayama

Prefecture, where you can explore the ancient Mount Koya, Kobe, the beautiful coastal town of the region, and then Tokyo. Exploring the area will allow you to immerse yourself in Japanese culture and see other parts of this archipelago rather than simply sticking to Kyoto.

What to Do in the Kansai Region

Nara

The beautiful, ancient city of Nara is filled with historical significance in Japan. Nara was the country's original capital, and the first emperor ascended the throne in 710. This city has plenty of things to explore, including several UNESCO World Heritage sites, such as Todai-ji Temple, which has one of the biggest Buddha statues, and the Kasuga Taisha Shrine, lined with stone lanterns. The nearby Nara Park is also a popular attraction, as you can mingle with friendly deer roaming the green space. Crackers to feed the deer can be purchased around the park, making it a lovely opportunity for a family outing.

Osaka

Osaka is the third-largest city in Japan, with plenty of things to do and immerse yourself in. Osaka is well-known for its food scene, with the Dotonbori district standing out as a haven for foodies. Visiting this district will give you a chance to taste many iconic dishes from various street vendors and restaurants, including *takoyaki* (octopus balls), *okonomiyaki* (pancakes), and *kushikatsu* (deep-fried skewers). The neon-lit alleys are also Gilco Running Man and Kani Doraku Crab signs, adding to the district's vibrant life.

Among the historical landmarks to explore in Osaka is the Osaka Castle, another symbol of Japan's feudal past. While the building standing tall today is a reconstruction of the former building from the 1620s, you can visit the museum to learn about Osaka Castle's history. Additionally, you can walk through Osaka Castle Park or enjoy a picnic in the green space while taking in the scenery. This park is also popular during the cherry blossom season.

If you're looking for entertainment, Osaka is where you can take in the thrills at Universal Studios Japan. There are ten theme parks to enjoy, including The Wizarding World of Harry Potter, Super Nintendo World, and Jurassic Park. Universal Studios Japan is open between 9 a.m. and 8 p.m., and the admission fees can vary depending on when you plan to visit the park:

- General admission (12 to 64 years old): ¥8400 to ¥9400
- Children (4 to 11 years old): ¥5400 to ¥6300
- Seniors (65 years old and up): ¥7600 to ¥8500

Mount Koya

Mount Koya, also known as Koyasan, is one of the most sacred places in the Kansai region. This mountain is located in the Wakayama Prefecture and is the main point of Shingon Buddhism. According to legend, this area was founded in 826 by Kobo Daishi, who chose the secluded mountaintop for spiritual practice and meditation.

Thus, he opened the Garan Temple when he found the lush, forested area atop Mount Koya.

One of the first things you should plan while in Mount Koya is to go and explore the numerous sacred sites, one of which is the Okunoin, the largest cemetery in Japan with over 200,000 tombstones of monks, feudal lords, and other important Japanese figures. As you hike toward Okunoin, you will also come across the Hall of Lamps (Torodo Hall), the main worship hall. It's stunning at night when the lanterns are lit, creating a beautiful glow.

This area is steeped in religious tradition and history, giving you a unique opportunity to immerse yourself in a spiritual journey or a deep cultural part of Japan. Mount Koya has a few traditional Buddhist temple lodgings to provide an immersive experience of the world of Buddhist practice and monastic life. Your stay will often include opportunities to join morning prayers and rituals, eat shojin ryori (a Buddhist vegetarian dish), and join meditation sessions led by residential monks.

Kobe

Kobe is one of Japan's most attractive cities, given its location along Osaka Bay and Mount Rokko. The city once played a significant role as a major port when the Port of Kobe opened in 1868.

This city has plenty of areas to explore, including the scenic harbor, where you can watch the port activity as you stroll along the waterfront or while enjoying a meal at one of the restaurants that overlook the harbor. Speaking of culinary delights, Kobe is famous for its Kobe beef, which is so tender it will melt in your mouth.

To explore some historical parts of Kobe that will give you a glimpse into its merchants, visit the Kitano-cho district. Here, several museums display antique furniture from previous foreign merchant residents. There is a small fee to enter these museums (between ¥500 and ¥750), but you can buy combination tickets if you plan to visit a few of the merchant houses.

If you want to take panoramic views of Kobe, Osaka Bay, and Awaji Island (seen on clear days), it is worth taking a cable car, the ropeway, or bus to the summit of Mount Rokko. This is also a popular place to visit if you want to explore hiking opportunities and enjoy nature. Other attractions on the mountain range include a garden, a music box museum, and a sheep pasture. If you take the bus, it can connect you to the various small attractions on the mountain.

Another notable attraction to check out in Kobe is the Akashi Kaikyo Bridge. This impressive suspension bridge is the longest globally, spanning 2.4 miles to connect Kobe to Awaji Island. One neat way to experience this bridge is by walking the platform under it along the Maiko Marine Promenade. This allows you to see the interior of the bridge while taking in the views of Osaka Bay and the Akashi Strait.

You can do a lot in this port city and don't need to break the bank to do it! Kobe is perfect for days of meandering without a plan.

Where to Eat in Kyoto and the Kansai Region

Torisei—Kyoto Tower Sando Branch

Address: 721-1, Higashishio-Koji Cho, Karasuma Dori Shichijo Sagaru, Shimogyo-ku, Kyoto-shi, Kyoto 600-8216

Hours of operation: 11 a.m. to 11 p.m. daily

Torisei Kyoto Tower Sando Branch is renowned for its delicious take on Japanese cuisine. This low-budget restaurant offers diverse dishes using the freshest ingredients from the Miyagi Prefecture. One of the most popular menu options is the *yakitori*, a skewer of chicken topped with a house-made sauce using sake.

Aragawa

Address: 2-15-18 Nakayamate-dori, Kobe, Hyogo-ken 650-0004

Hours of operation: 12 p.m. and 3 p.m., 5 p.m. and 10 p.m. (closed on Sundays)

Aragawa is a great place to eat if you love steak. The steaks served at this restaurant come from a farm in Sanda and will melt in your mouth upon taking a bite. As you can expect, prices will be a little higher here, but worth every yen given how delicious every meal is.

Okonomiyaki Mizuno

Address: 1-4-15 Dotonbori, Chuo-ku, Osaka 542-0071

Hours of operation: 11 a.m. to 10 p.m. (closed on Thursdays)

Okonomiyaki Mizuno is a family-run business in its third generation. This restaurant offers okonomiyaki, a fluffy pancake cooked to perfection and topped or filled with meat, seafood, or vegetables. Okonomiyaki Mizuno is a popular establishment among the locals, and you can expect long lines, especially around lunch and dinner time; however, the line moves quickly.

Yuba Higashiyamayuuzu

Address: 570-218 Gionmachi Minamigawa, Higashiyama Ward, Kyoto, 605-0074

Hours of operation

- Lunch: 11 a.m. to 3 p.m. (last orders are taken at 2 p.m.)
- Dinner: 5:30 p.m. to 9:30 p.m. (last orders are taken at 8:30 p.m.)

Yuba Higashiyamayuuzu specializes in traditional Japanese cuisine and is a popular establishment where you can enjoy yuba dishes made from tofu skin. Eating at this establishment is a simple and elegant dining experience, with everything made using high-quality ingredients. This will enhance your experience while in Kyoto as you get a taste of Kyoto's culinary heritage.

Tsujiri Cafe

Address: 721-1 Higashishiokojicho, Shimogyo Ward, Kyoto, 600-8216

Hours of operation: 9 a.m. to 9 p.m.

Tsujiri Cafe is a popular place if you're craving sweet treats. This café is well-known for making matcha-based desserts and beverages, including matcha soft-serve ice cream and matcha tiramisu. You'll find this little cafe inside the Nidec Kyoto Tower.

What to Eat in the Kyoto and the Kassai Region

Kaiseki Ryori

Kaiseki Ryori is a traditional multi-course Japanese meal that originated in Kyoto. It features a meticulously crafted sequence of small, seasonal dishes that highlight the flavors and textures of local ingredients. Kaiseki meals often include fresh sashimi, grilled fish, simmered vegetables, and delicate desserts, presented with exquisite attention to detail.

Yudofu

Yudofu is a simple yet elegant dish made from simmered tofu served with dipping sauce and condiments. In Kyoto, yudofu is often enjoyed at traditional Japanese ryokan (inns) or specialized yudofu restaurants. The dish highlights the purity and delicate flavor of tofu, making it a popular choice for vegetarians and health-conscious diners.

Takoyaki

Takoyaki are delicious octopus-filled savory balls made from a batter of flour, eggs, and dashi broth. They are cooked in a special takoyaki pan, which gives them their signature round shape. Takoyaki is typically topped with takoyaki sauce, mayonnaise, bonito flakes, and dried seaweed flakes, creating a flavorful and satisfying snack or street food.

Kobe Beef

While technically not in Kyoto or the immediate Kansai region, Kobe Beef is a famous delicacy that is easily accessible from Kyoto and Osaka. Kobe Beef is renowned for its exceptional marbling, tenderness, and rich flavor. It is often served as a steak or in hotpot dishes like sukiyaki or shabu-shabu, allowing diners to savor its melt-in-your-mouth texture and exquisite taste.

Where to Stay in Kyoto and the Kansai Region

APA Hotel Kyoto Gion Excellent

Address: 555 Gionmachi Minamigawa, Higashiyama Ward, Kyoto 605-0074
APA Hotel Kyoto Gion Excellent is a three-star hotel in the Gion district. This hotel will give you easy access to several popular attractions in the area and the bustling streets of downtown Kyoto, including the Kyoto Imperial Palace.

Four Seasons Hotel Kyoto

Address: 445-3 Myohoin Maekawacho, Higashiyama Ward, Kyoto 605-0932
The Four Seasons Kyoto is a top luxury option thanks to its amenities and serene surroundings. This hotel is nestled around Shakusui-en, a pond dating back to the 12th century. The elegant rooms at this hotel feature traditional Japanese design elements. There is also free Wi-Fi, an indoor swimming pool, and spa facilities offering rejuvenating treatments.

Koyasan Shukubo Yochiin

Address: 293 Koyasan, Koya-cho, Ito-gun, Wakayama Prefecture 648-0211
If you want to stay at a Buddhist temple to immerse yourself in its practices, Koyasan Shukubo Yochiin is a budget-friendly option. This temple dates back to 1127 and allows you to experience Buddhist rituals and try the shojin ryori. All of the rooms are private, but the bathrooms are shared.

Sotetsu Fresa Inn Kobe Sannomiya

Address: 5 Chome-2-3 Asahidori, Chuo Ward, Kobe, Hyogo 651-0095
Sotetsu Fresa Inn Kobe Sannomiya is in the heart of the vibrant Chuo Ward. It provides easy access to transportation hubs, shopping districts, and dining

options, making exploring what Kobe offers convenient. Additionally, this hotel is steps from several of Kobe's attractions, including the Kobe Kitano Museum and Flower Road.

Santiago Guesthouse Kyoto

Address: 6-503 Yūgyōmaechō, Higashiyama Ward, Kyoto 605-0864

Santiago Guesthouse Kyoto is a budget-friendly option for those traveling solo or wanting hostel-type accommodation. You'll stay in a traditional wooden townhouse (*machiya*) at this guesthouse to provide a unique cultural experience. The room is a shared, mixed dormitory with a shared lounge and a café.

What Not to Do in Kyoto and the Kansai Region

Don't Take Subways and Taxis Everywhere in Kyoto

When visiting different regions of Kyoto, don't feel the need to rely on taxis or public transportation to get you from one place to the next. Once in the area you plan to explore, you can easily walk from one place to the next. Only public transport can get to different parts of the city, from the northern area to the southern part of Kyoto.

Don't Just Book Any Accommodation

Depending on what you want to do in this part of Japan, deciding where to stay for the night will be necessary. If you intend to visit the shrines and temples, your best bet is to stay in Kyoto. On the other hand, if you want to explore the Kansai region, pick an accommodation near public transportation so you can conveniently travel to where you want to explore.

Don't Disrespect Geisha Culture

Although only a handful of geishas are still around today, don't disrespect and approach them. They are still working and deserve the respect of being able to move around to their different engagements without being interrupted by a tourist for a selfie.

Don't Try to climb on the Pavilion at Kinkaku-ji.

Kinkaku-ji is a UNESCO World Heritage Site and an important cultural and religious symbol in Japan. While the Golden Pavilion is a stunning sight to behold, it is also a fragile structure. Climbing on or touching the pavilion is strictly prohibited to preserve its integrity and protect its golden exterior.

Respect Fox Statues at Fushimi Inari Taisha

Foxes, or "kitsune," are considered messengers of Inari and are often depicted throughout the shrine grounds. Visitors should avoid touching or defacing fox statues, as they are revered symbols of the shrine's religious significance. Fushimi Inari is famous for its thousands of vermilion torii gates that form a network of trails leading up Mount Inari. While it may be tempting to climb or lean on the gates for photos, visitors should refrain from doing so.

Beware of crowding at Arashiyama Bamboo Groove.

The Arashiyama Bamboo Grove can get crowded, especially during peak tourist seasons. Visitors should be mindful of others around them and avoid blocking pathways or stopping abruptly to take photos. While the bamboo grove is an incredible sight to behold, visitors should refrain from touching or damaging the bamboo stalks. The bamboo grove is known for its peaceful atmosphere, and loud noise can disrupt the serenity of the surroundings.

Don't Skip Jishu Shrine at Kiyomizu-dera Temple

Jishu Shrine, located within the Kiyomizu-dera complex, is dedicated to the deity of love and matchmaking. Visitors should take the time to explore this unique shrine and participate in its rituals for good luck in love. While the temple complex offers stunning views and unique architecture, visitors should refrain from climbing on or touching structures to preserve their integrity and ensure safety.

Don't Feed Deer at Nara

Nara is famous for its free-roaming deer, which are considered sacred messengers of the gods in the Shinto religion. While it's tempting to feed or interact with them, travelers should avoid aggressive behavior and follow guidelines for feeding provided by local authorities.

Next Stop: Hiroshima and the Chugoku Region

Kyoto has plenty of things to see and do, especially since it has over 3,000 shrines and temples within its city. In this chapter, we looked at the various things to do while in Kyoto, including some of the iconic landmarks like the Imperial Palace and some of the festivals to immerse yourself in Japanese culture. In the next chapter, we will explore the Hiroshima and Chugoku region, where you can immerse yourself in some of the most turbulent moments while exploring some of the landmarks that have shaped the city and region's past.

Chapter 6:

Hiroshima and the Chugoku Region—Dos and Don'ts

H iroshima has plenty of history to unfold, especially with the devastating effects of the atomic bomb dropped by the US in World War II. As a reminder of Hiroshima's resilience, the Peace Bell in Hiroshima Memorial Park is a poignant reminder of the devastating consequences of war. Many people who visit this iconic bell will ring it, allowing the chimes to echo throughout the park as people commit to unite to keep peace among nations while remembering the lives lost on that impactful day in the world's history.

Discovering Hiroshima

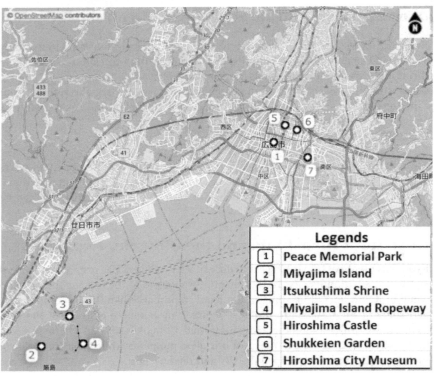

	Legends
1	Peace Memorial Park
2	Miyajima Island
3	Itsukushima Shrine
4	Miyajima Island Ropeway
5	Hiroshima Castle
6	Shukkeien Garden
7	Hiroshima City Museum

Hiroshima is one city that remains heavy in history, especially when the atomic bomb was dropped on the city on August 6, 1945, killing millions of people. Despite the tragedy that unfolded, this beautiful city doesn't hold bitterness about what happened but continues to move forward and work to bring people together in harmony.

When you visit Hiroshima, you will experience a different atmosphere than in other parts of Japan. This, of course, will be notable in the historical landmarks, such as the Hiroshima Peace Memorial Park, dedicated to commemorating the victims of the atomic bombing. The Atomic Bomb Dome, another UNESCO World Heritage site, also stands as a reminder of what the city went through in 1945.

Beyond its sad history, Hiroshima is lively and vibrant. There is much to explore throughout the city, including Hiroshima Castle and the Shukkeien Garden—plenty of festivals to immerse yourself in and a diverse culinary experience for any taste bud to feast upon.

Whatever you decide to do in Hiroshima, this city will move you and teach you new life lessons. Be open to the lessons as you take in the culture and beautiful sights, enjoy the food, and learn to embrace the city's hopeful future.

What to Do in Hiroshima

Hiroshima Peace Memorial Park

Hiroshima Peace Memorial Park is a tribute to the victims of the tragic bombing during World War II. This beautiful green space was established to honor the lives that were lost and to promote peace. As you explore this lovely green space, you will see several monuments and memorials commemorating August 6, 1945. The park's centerpiece is the Peace Memorial Museum, which includes a chronicle of events that led up to the bombing and the aftermath. Visiting this museum can be upsetting for some visitors, but it is also a stark reminder not to take peace for granted.

In addition to visiting the museum, it is worth visiting the Atomic Bomb Dome, which was Hiroshima's former Prefectural Industrial Promotion Hall. When the US dropped the atomic bomb, impressively, this building didn't collapse, allowing you to explore the remains of the war. There is also an arched tomb called the Cenotaph, which can be found between the A-Bomb Dome and Peace Memorial Museum. The Cenotaph has a list of victims who died when the bomb exploded or from radiation exposure.

Visiting this park will allow you to reflect upon the devastating impact of nuclear warfare while also witnessing Hiroshima's commitment to peace and reconciliation.

Peace Memorial Museum

Hours of operation

- March to July: 7:30 a.m. to 7 p.m.
- August: 7:30 a.m. to 8 p.m. (August 5 and 6 have extended hours to 9 p.m.)
- September to November: 7:30 a.m. to 7 p.m.
- December to February: 7:30 a.m. to 6 p.m.
- The museum is closed on December 30 and 31.
- The last admission is 30 minutes before closing time.

Ticket type	Price
Adults	¥200
High school students	¥100
Junior high school students and younger	Free

Miyajima Island

Miyajima Island is about an hour away by train and ferry from Hiroshima. This island is renowned for its stunning natural beauty and the iconic Itsukushima Shrine, a UNESCO World Heritage site famous for its torii gate that appears floating on the water when the tide is in. If you are there when the tide is out, you can get up close to the Torii gate and take some great photos. In addition to exploring the gate, there are several buildings you can explore at the shrine, all of which are connected by a boardwalk over the water. As you explore the buildings, it is recommended to buy a combined ticket to see the treasure hall displaying thousands of different items and artifacts, including armory, instruments, and Noh masks.

Beyond the shrine, Miyajima Island is a haven for outdoor enthusiasts who love hiking. The peak of Mount Misen is 500 meters above sea level, offering fantastic views of the Seto Inland Sea; if it's a clear day, you'll be able to see as far as Hiroshima. You can take three trails to the top: the Momijidani, Daisho-in, and Omoto. Depending on your fitness level, reaching the top of any path will take about two hours. If you're not up to hiking, a ropeway goes up the mountain, where you can take in the views from the observation deck.

Itsukushima Shrine

Shrine hours of operation

- January 1: 12 a.m. to 6: 30 p.m.
- January 2 and 3: 6:30 a.m. to 6:30 p.m.
- January 4 to February: 6:30 a.m. to 5:30 p.m.
- March to October 14: 6:30 a.m. to 6 p.m.
- October 15 to November: 6:30 a.m. to 5:30 p.m.
- December: 6:30 p.m. to 5 p.m.

Treasure Hall hours of operation: 8 a.m. to 5 p.m. daily

Ticket type	Itsukushima Shrine	Treasure Hall	Combined ticket
Adult	¥300	¥300	¥500
High school students	¥200	¥200	¥300
Junior high school and elementary school students	¥100	¥100	¥150

Miyajima Island Ropeway

Hours of operation

- Going up: 9 a.m. to 4 p.m. daily
- Going down: 9:20 a.m. to 4:20 p.m. daily

Ticket type	One way	Round trip
Adult	¥1100	¥2000
Child	¥550	¥1000

Hiroshima Castle

Address: 21-1 Motomachi, Naka Ward, Hiroshima 730-0011

Hours of operation: 9 a.m. to 6 p.m. daily

Hiroshima Castle dates back to 1589 when the powerful feudal lord Mori Terumoto had it constructed. It played a significant role in the region's governance and served as an economic center for Hiroshima. Unfortunately, the original castle was destroyed during the atomic bombing of Hiroshima on August 6, 1945.

Following the war and bombing, the castle's main keep was rebuilt in 1958 to replicate the appearance of the original castle. Inside, you can explore the museum exhibits showcasing Hiroshima's history, the castle's history, and the reconstruction efforts. The museum also features the history of some of Japan's other castles. The top floor of the castle offers panoramic views of Hiroshima as well.

You must pay to go to the main keep, but wandering the castle grounds is free.

Ticket type	Price
Adults	¥370
High school students and seniors	¥180
Junior high school students	¥100

Shukkeien Garden

Address: 2-11 Kaminoborichō, Naka Ward, Hiroshima 730-0014

Hours of operation

- March 16 to September 15: 9 a.m. to 6 p.m. daily
- September 16 to March 15: 9 a.m. to 7 p.m. daily
- The last admission is 30 minutes before the garden closes.

Shukkeien Garden is an excellent example of a traditional Japanese garden with a long history dating back to 1620. *Shukkeien*, which translates to "shrunken-scenery garden," has a beautiful pond in the middle with pathways and a bridge surrounding it. This garden has a path that winds around the pond and passes through many different sceneries. You may also want to stop into one of the tea houses to enjoy a cup of matcha or green tea while enjoying the garden's tranquility.

Ticket type	Price
Adults	¥260
High school and university students	¥150
Elementary and junior high school students	¥100

Hiroshima City Museum of Contemporary Art

Address: X1-1 Hijiyamakōen, Minami Ward, Hiroshima 732-0815

Hours of operation: 10 a.m. to 5 p.m. The last admission is at 4:30 p.m. The museum is closed on Sundays and Mondays.

The Hiroshima City Museum of Contemporary Art should be on your visit list, especially if you are a big fan of art. This museum opened its doors in May 1989 and features more than 300 works of contemporary art from Japanese and international artists. In addition to the permanent collection, the museum has exhibitions that rotate regularly, offering you the chance to see new and thought-provoking art.

The building is also an exciting piece of architecture. It was designed by renowned architect Kisho Kurokawa, who integrated the museum's architecture into its natural surroundings. As you explore the museum's exhibits, take note of the transition in materials: It starts with natural stone, then changes to tiles, and finally finishes with aluminum. This progression symbolizes the evolution of craftsmanship and civilization and its changes.

Ticket type	Price
Adults	¥500
Seniors (65 years old and up)	¥400
College students	¥320
High school students and younger	Free

What Events to Enjoy in Hiroshima

Hiroshima Peace Memorial Ceremony

The Hiroshima Peace Memorial Ceremony is held annually on August 6 in Hiroshima Peace Memorial Park. This ceremony begins at around 8 a.m. with a moment of silence. At 8:15 a.m., the exact time when the bomb detonated over Hiroshima, sirens will sound around the city as the Peace Bell is rung. This ceremony also includes speeches and prayers of peace. Many will also send lit lanterns down the river. This tradition began during World War II by the survivors of the atomic bombing. This ceremony, though somber, is an opportunity to reflect with others on the tragedy and a way to join in on the unified vision of a world without nuclear weapons.

Hiroshima Flower Festival

The Hiroshima Flower Festival is a vibrant three-day event on Hiroshima's Peace Boulevard. This event has been around for 40 years and features various activities, including parades and performances on multiple stages set up along the road. The final day of the Hiroshima Festival is the most popular day to go as many performance teams dance the Yosaki dance while parading down Peace Boulevard. Beyond the fun and vibrant atmosphere of the festival, it aims to deliver a message of peace through flowers while bringing everyone together.

Hiroshima Carp Baseball Games

While baseball is a favorite pastime in the US, it is also a very popular sport in Japan. So, if you want to enjoy a sporting event while on your trip, it is worth watching The Carp, Hiroshima's professional baseball team that competes in the Central League of Nippon Professional Baseball (NPB). The home games happen at the Mazda Zoom-Zoom Stadium, and the atmosphere is unlike anything you would encounter at a Major League Baseball (MLB) game. Fans go wild as they cheer for their favorite players, and you can expect to see some intense on-field action. It's a fun way to spend an afternoon or evening and experience baseball in another country!

Discovering the Chugoku Region

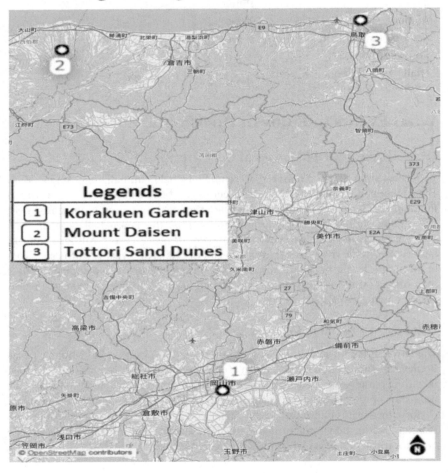

Outside of Hiroshima, one of the more significant cities in the Chugoku Region, there is much more to discover in this part of Japan. Okayama is famous for Okayama Castle and the beautiful Korakuen Garden, which is adjacent to the historic castle and is considered one of Japan's three greatest gardens. In the Tottori district, you can explore the Tottori Sand Dunes, stretch your legs, and exercise while hiking the dormant volcano Mount Daison. As Hiroshima is a famous city, you will find the other prefectures in Chugoku to be less busy, making your travels more enjoyable.

What to Do in the Chugoku Region

Okayama's Korakuen Garden

Address: 1-5 Kōrakuen, Kita Ward, Okayama 703-8257
Hours of operation: 8 a.m. to 5 p.m. daily

Okayama's Korakuen Garden is another of Japan's Three Great Gardens, with a stunning landscape spanning over 32 acres. The history of this garden dates back to the late 1680s when feudal lord Ikeda Tsunamasa ordered it to be made a place to entertain guests. The garden did not open until the mid-1880s after the feudal era ended.

Today, guests can explore the expansive garden space by following the winding paths around the large pond and streams and the grove lined with cherry, plum, and maple trees. The garden also contains historic buildings, which are worth admiring.

Ticket type	Price
Adults (19 years old and up)	¥410
Senor (64 years old and up)	¥140
Children up to 18 years old	Free

Mount Daisen

If you are seeking outdoor adventures, visit Mount Daisen. This dormant volcano is in the Tottori region and is 1,729 meters above sea level. Visiting this mountain will offer you a wide range of hiking trails with different difficulty levels and distances, allowing you to take in the breathtaking views of the surrounding landscape. Another trail worth exploring is the Daisendaki Waterfall trail, which will bring you through lush forests to a stunning two-tiered waterfall.

The mountain is also famous for skiers and snowboarders who want to challenge themselves down the slopes at the Daisen White Resort. There are black diamond ski runs and bunny slopes for beginners. Snowshoeing tours are also available in the winter.

Tottori Sand Dunes

The Tottori Sand Dunes offer a unique desert-like scene in the Tottori region. Spanning about three miles along the Sea of Japan, these dunes were formed thousands of years ago when the sand from the Sendaigawa River washed out to sea and then was deposited along the coast by the Sea of Japan. Naturally, as the dunes' have a unique geography, there are plenty of opportunities for outdoor activities, such as sandboarding (similar to snowboarding), paragliding, and camel or horse-drawn cart rides. An observation deck at the Sakyu Center will give you great views of the dunes from up high.

Where to Eat in Hiroshima and the Chugoku Region

Denko-Sekka Ekimae-Hiroba

Address: 6F Full Focus Building, 10-1 Matsubara-cho, Minami-Ku, Hiroshima City, Hiroshima Prefecture 732-0822

Hours of operation: 10 a.m. to 11:30 p.m. daily

Denko-Sekka Ekimae-Hiroba is a great place to pop into for lunch or dinner before continuing to explore Hiroshima. At this establishment, you can choose from a wide range of options made available to you. Some popular choices are their okonomiyaki and teppanyaki dishes made with oyster or Momiji pork, and you can expect the menu prices to be relatively low.

Sawatdee Lemongrass Grill

Address: 5-2 Horikawacho, Mashinakaku, Hiroshima, Hiroshima Prefecture 730-0033

Hours of operation

- Lunch service
    - Monday, Wednesday to Friday from 11 a.m. to 2:30 p.m. (last chance to order is at 2 p.m.)
    - Saturday, Sunday, and holidays from 11 a.m. to 3 p.m. (last chance to order is at 2:30 p.m.)
- Dinner service
    - Monday, Wednesday, Thursday from 5 p.m. to 10 p.m.
    - Friday and Saturday from 5 p.m. to 10:30 p.m.
    - Sunday from 5 p.m. to 10 p.m.

If you want to indulge in Thai cuisine, Sawatdee Lemongrass Grill offers a great selection of Thai-inspired dishes. This restaurant is cheap, even for a course with several Thai dishes. You can expect menu items such as pad thai if you pop in for lunch.

Azuma Sushi Sun Station Terrace Okayama

Address: 1-1 Ekimotomachi, Kita-ku Sun Ste Okayama South Bldg. 2F, Okayama, Okayama Prefecture 700-0024

Hours of operation: 11 a.m. to 10 p.m. daily

Azuma Sushi Sun Station Terrace Okayama is a top place to eat in the Chugoku region if you want to indulge in sushi dishes. This restaurant serves sushi and nigiri rolls made with high-quality fish and ingredients. It can be pretty busy, especially in the evenings, but it is worth the wait, given how delicious everything is!

Udon Chiyoshi

Address: 2-4-5 Karochominami, Tottori, Tottori Prefecture 680-0909

Hours of operation: 10:30 a.m. to 9 p.m. daily

If you crave an udon noodle-based dish, check out Udon Chiyoshi in Tottori. This establishment's menu features a variety of udon dishes, some served in broth and others with teppanyaki. The prices are pretty cheap, and you can customize your dish to include whatever you want.

Teppanyaki Naniwa

Address: 6-78, Moto-machi, Naka-ku, Hiroshima city, Hiroshima 730-0011

Hours of operation
Lunch: 11:30 a.m. to 2:30 p.m. (last order is at 2 p.m.), Dinner: 5:30 p.m. to 9:30 p.m. (last order is at 9 p.m.)

Teppanyaki Naniwa is a dining experience you can enjoy while in Hiroshima. At this restaurant, you will watch Chef Matsubara work magic creating delicious Japanese dishes using high-quality Hiroshima beef, seafood, and seasonal vegetables. This is a bit more expensive, but the interactive experience makes it worth it.

What to Eat in Hiroshima and the Chugoku Region

Hiroshima-style Okonomiyaki

Hiroshima is famous for its take on okonomiyaki, a savory pancake made with layers of cabbage, noodles, and various toppings. Unlike the Osaka-style okonomiyaki, which mixes all ingredients together, Hiroshima-style okonomiyaki layers them on the grill, resulting in a distinct texture and flavor. It's typically topped with okonomiyaki sauce, mayonnaise, bonito flakes, and dried seaweed.

Hiroshima-style Tsukemen

Tsukemen is a type of ramen where the noodles are served separately from the broth, allowing diners to dip them into a rich and flavorful broth before slurping them up. Hiroshima-style tsukemen is known for its thick and chewy noodles, accompanied by a dipping sauce made from soy sauce, fish broth, and various seasonings. It's a hearty and satisfying dish that's perfect for dipping on a chilly day.

Hiroshima-style Oysters

Hiroshima is renowned for its fresh and succulent oysters, which are harvested from the nearby Seto Inland Sea. Visitors to the region can enjoy oysters in various forms, including raw, grilled, fried, or in hotpot dishes like kaki-nabe. Hiroshima-style oysters are prized for their plumpness and sweetness, making them a must-try for seafood lovers.

Izakaya-style Dishes

Izakayas are casual Japanese pubs where locals gather to enjoy drinks and small dishes. In the Chugoku region, you'll find a wide variety of izakaya-style dishes, including yakitori (grilled skewers), karaage (fried chicken), sashimi (raw fish), and more. These dishes are perfect for sharing with friends and sampling a variety of flavors.

Where to Stay in Hiroshima and the Chugoku Region

Kifuno Sato

Address: 180 Yunogō, Mimasaka, Okayama 707-0062

Staying at Kifuno Sato will be an experience in itself as it is located in the historic hot spring district in Yunogō. This inn is a traditional ryokan, but large private open-air baths are in the rooms overlooking the garden. Kifuno Sato also has a medicinal stone sauna, which is apparently great for detoxifying and improving your skin. This is a bit more luxurious, but given its place in Okayama, it's worth it even for a night!

Hiroshima Washington Hotel

Address: 2-7 Shintenchi, Naka Ward, Hiroshima 730-0034

Hiroshima Washington Hotel is a three-star accommodation in the bustling Hondori district. It is a great option if you want to be closer to Hiroshima's exciting nightlife. It is also a short walk from Hiroshima Peace Memorial Park and Hiroshima Castle. Several room options are available, all of which are of a decent size. There is also a breakfast buffet you can take advantage of in the mornings.

The Knot Hiroshima

Address: 3 Chome-1-1 Otemachi, Naka Ward, Hiroshima 730-0051

The Knot Hiroshima is a four-star hotel in a prime position near Hiroshima Peace Memorial Park. This hotel has a stylish interior that makes you feel like you've entered a New York building. Free Wi-Fi is offered throughout the hotel and in the rooms. If you're looking to eat, a restaurant in the hotel serves food throughout the day, with pizza being a top menu choice. There is also a rooftop bar where you can enjoy a cocktail while taking in the sites of downtown Hiroshima on the warm summer nights.

Comfort Hotel Hiroshima Otemachi

Address: 3 Chome-7-9 Ōtemachi, Naka Ward, Hiroshima 730-0051

The Comfort Hotel Hiroshima Otemachi is a convenient and affordable accommodation in the downtown area of Hiroshima. This three-star hotel has some great perks, including nightwear, slippers, and toothbrush sets in the rooms. There is also a complimentary breakfast serving Japanese and Western-style cuisine in the mornings. Free Wi-Fi is also provided throughout the hotel and in rooms.

Hotel Granvia Hiroshima

Address: 1-5 Matsubarachō, Minami Ward, Hiroshima 732-0822

Hotel Granvia Hiroshima is another three-star hotel in Hiroshima. It is conveniently adjacent to the Hiroshima Shinkansen station, making it easy to access transportation links to other parts of the city, including Hiroshima Memorial Park, Hiroshima Castle, and Mazda Zoom-Zoom Stadium. The rooms in this hotel are modern and have fridges. There are also six restaurants offering a range of Japanese and international cuisines.

What Not to Do in Hiroshima and the Chugoku Region

Don't Avoid Hiroshima

Hiroshima was the site of the first use of an atomic weapon against a population. On the 6th of August 1945, the bomb was dropped on the center of Hiroshima, causing massive destruction and loss of life. Although this may seem like an odd place for a tourist to visit, it is worth a trip. The museum has information and artifacts, as well as eyewitness accounts. The Japanese feel it's extremely important to remember the effect war can have on a population and want people to visit.

To balance the haunting atmosphere of the museum, the park outside is peaceful and beautiful. There are thousands of origami cranes dotted around, which people make to remember those affected by the bombs. Don't avoid Hiroshima; it is well worth the trip.

Don't Take Pictures in the Peace Memorial Museum

If you visit the Peace Memorial Museum, refrain from taking photos of the exhibits. Remember, this museum serves as a reminder of what Hiroshima and Japan endured during World War II, and not taking pictures shows utmost respect for the city.

Don't Be Insensitive About World War II

World War II was devastating around the globe. However, remember that Japan has its own set of cultural sensitivities around what happened, especially when the atomic bomb detonated. As you explore the Hiroshima Peace Memorial Park and museum, remember to respect the history and don't start blaming anyone for what happened.

Respect Flora and Fauna at Shukkeien Garden

Shukkeien Garden is a meticulously landscaped garden with carefully manicured plants, trees, and water features. Travelers should refrain from picking flowers, climbing trees, or disturbing the natural environment in any way. While there may be bridges and other structures within Shukkeien Garden, travelers should refrain from climbing on them or engaging in any behavior that could damage or disrupt these features.

Check Weather Conditions before venturing into Tottori Sand Dunes.

The sand dunes can be exposed to harsh weather conditions, including strong winds, high temperatures, and sandstorms. Check the weather forecast before visiting and take appropriate precautions, such as wearing sunscreen, staying hydrated, and seeking shelter during inclement weather. Some areas of the sand dunes may be off-limits to visitors to protect sensitive habitats or prevent erosion. Respect any signage or barriers indicating restricted access and refrain from climbing in prohibited areas. While sandboarding is a popular activity at the Tottori Sand Dunes, be sure to do so only in designated areas where it is permitted. Sandboarding in prohibited areas can damage sensitive habitats and pose safety risks to both visitors and wildlife.

Next Stop: The Tohoku Region

A visit to Hiroshima will leave a lasting impact, given its history with World War II. However, despite the city's somber past, there is much to see, learn, and explore while in this part of Japan. Outside of Hiroshima, there is more adventure to be had in places like Totorri and Okayama. From visiting this region, you'll have a deeper understanding of a country with strong resilience and a desire to unite people without violence.

With much more of Japan left to see, we will explore the Tohoku region, which has plenty of rugged beauty. This is an excellent region for those keen on outdoor adventures over the hustle and bustle of city life.

Chapter 7:

The Tohuku Region—Dos and Don'ts

T he Tohoku region is situated on the northeastern side of Japan and has an interesting fact attached to it. Despite being considered a cold region given its geographical location, Tohoku is surprisingly the top strawberry producer in the country—even when it snows. That's because the Tohoku farmers use greenhouses to foster the right environment to grow these delicious berries so they can thrive despite the weather outside. In addition to being a haven for growing strawberries, Tohoku is a top fruit producer, growing apples, pears, and cherries throughout the year. There are many delicious fruits to enjoy in this region, among other exciting things, so let's get into it!

Discovering the Tohoku Region

The Tohoku region is the country's main island and comprises six prefectures: Aomori, Iwate, Miyagi, Akita, Yamagata, and Fukushima.

Culturally rich, Tohoku is home to numerous traditional festivals, crafts, and culinary dishes that reflect this part of Japan's deep-rooted heritage. From the famous Soma Nomaoi festival celebrating the samurai heritage to the interesting craftsmanship and stories behind the Kokeshi dolls made in Miyagi, this region also holds historical significance, as evidenced by sites like the temples in Hiraizumi and in the former samurai town, Kakunodate.

Tohoku's geography is a haven for outdoor enthusiasts who want to enjoy many outdoor activities and explore diverse landscapes. These include following the many hiking trails in Towada-Hachimantai National Park, skiing in Iwate, and taking in the sights at Matsushima Bay in Miyagi.

Whatever way you choose to explore the Tohoku region, you will uncover much more of Japan's storied past, take in the breathtaking landscape, and find ways to immerse yourself in Japan's rich culture.

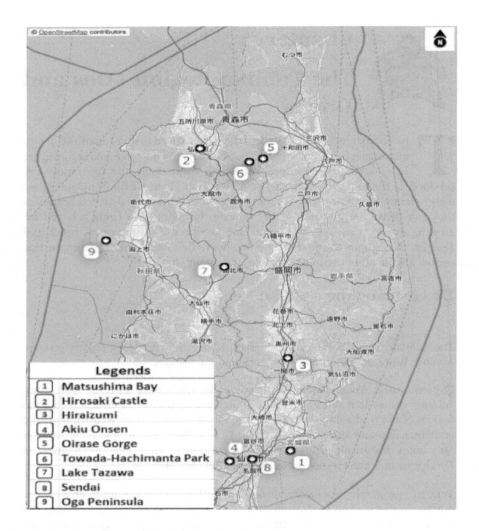

Legends

1	Matsushima Bay
2	Hirosaki Castle
3	Hiraizumi
4	Akiu Onsen
5	Oirase Gorge
6	Towada-Hachimanta Park
7	Lake Tazawa
8	Sendai
9	Oga Peninsula

What to Do in the Tohoku Region

Matsushima Bay

Matsushima Bay is near the Miyagi Prefecture and is celebrated as one of Japan's most scenic destinations. This is one of the best places to go in Tohoku to take in the outdoors and the surrounding landscape, as the bay is dotted with around 260 islands, all varying in size and dotted with many pine trees. One of the best ways to see these islands is to join a boat cruise that will take you around and provide commentary about the bay's history and significance to enhance your overall experience. Several companies offer cruises between ¥1500 and ¥2000 per person.

You can easily access three of Matsushima's islands on foot, thanks to the footbridges connected to the mainland. If you venture to the central island, you'll find the Godaido Temple, a landmark in Matsushima dating back to 1604. If you head over to Fukuura Island, you'll walk a long red bridge, and for a small fee, you can explore the forest and follow various pathways offering great views of the bay and the Benzaiten Temple. The other island you can reach by foot is Oshima Island, where you will find meditation caves with hand-carved markings and shoginan ruins.

The other temples to explore in Matsushima Bay include Zuiganji Temple, a Zen temple dating back to 1609. As you approach this temple, the path is lined with tall, beautiful cedar trees, enhancing its serene atmosphere. If you want to go into this temple, it is ¥700 and is open at 8:30 a.m. daily and closes at 5 p.m. between April and September, 4:30 p.m. in March and October, 4 p.m. in February and November, and 3:30 p.m. between January and December.

Hirosaki Castle and Park

Address: 1 Shimoshiroganecho, Hirosaki, Aomori Prefecture 036-8551

Hours of operation

- Castle

    o Mid-April to November 23: 9 a.m. to 5 p.m. (last admission is at 4:30 p.m.)

    o Closed from November 24 to March 31

- Garden

    o 9 a.m. to 5 p.m. (the last admission is at 4:30 p.m.)

    o Closed from November 24 to mid-April

Hirosaki Castle is one of the most historic castles in Japan, with its original building dating back to 1611. Unfortunately, it burnt down in 1627 after it was struck by lightning and was not rebuilt until 1810. It is the only castle that was not reconstructed when the country became more modernized.

You can explore this castle's three-story building and beautiful Japanese architecture. Additionally, the surrounding parkland is one of the best places to view the cherry blossom trees, as there are over 2,500 of them. The castle holds a festival every year between April 23 and May 5, when the trees are in full bloom, giving you another opportunity to immerse yourself in Japanese culture.

Ticket type	Hirosaki Castle only	Hirosaki Castle Garden only	Combined ticket
Adult	¥320	¥320	¥520
Child	¥100	¥100	¥160

Hiraizumi

Hiraizumi is one of Japan's most important historic towns, dating back to the 12th century. In this town, you can explore five UNESCO World Heritage sites, including the famous Chuson-ji and Motsu-ji temples. At Chuson-ji, you'll find the famous Konjikido Golden Hall, several Buddhist statues, and other exciting decor. After exploring the hall, it is worth visiting the storehouse, where you can view other artifacts that will give you a deeper insight into the temple's historical significance.

At the Motsu-ji Temple, you can explore the grounds and the surrounding gardens, symbolizing a Buddhist paradise. In addition to the tranquil ponds and lush vegetation, you can explore the ruins and foundations of the former temple, join a Zazen sitting meditation, and enjoy ennen-cha tea.

Aside from these two temples, there are other ruins and gardens to explore. To take in as much of the town as possible, spending at least half a day here is a good idea.

Akiu Onsen

Address: 7-1, Kidoho, Yumoto, Akiu-machi, Taihaku-ku, Sendai-shi, Miyagi 982-0241

Hours of operation

- Public and garden baths: 5 a.m. to 9 a.m. and 11 a.m. to 1 p.m. The last entrance is at 8:30 a.m., as the facility will close at 9 a.m. until 11 a.m. for cleaning.
- Hot springs: 11 a.m. to 5 p.m. (closed on Tuesdays).

It never hurts to indulge in self-care, even while on vacation. Akiu Onsen is one of the most famous hot spring resorts, renowned for its chloride water. This resort dates back 1,500 years and was once a royal bathhouse. It is open to the public today, and you can soak in its therapeutic waters.

Ticket type	Price
Adult	¥900
Junior high school students	¥830
Elementary school students	¥500

Oirase Gorge

Oirase Gorge is a scenic hike in the Aomori Prefecture. This beautiful hike is about 8.6 miles, with the stunning river weaving through the dense forest with cascading waterfalls. This hike is one of the most popular in the fall due to the foliage turning vibrant shades of red, orange, and yellow. It is easily one of the most enchanting and tranquil hikes to do in Tohoku, especially if you are an outdoorsy person!

Towada-Hachimantai National Park

For another outdoor adventure in the Tohoku region, visit the Towada-Hachimantai National Park. This national park spans the Aomori and Akita Prefectures. It boasts many hikes to explore the diverse landscapes, including the volcanic terrain of Akita-Komagatake and Mount Hakkoda and the beautiful shores along Lake Towada. Hiking in this national park will bring you through lush forests, past cascading waterfalls, and more. This is another popular place to visit in the fall due to the foliage changing to vibrant orange, yellow, and red hues.

This national park also has several hot springs you can explore and try out. Among the most popular ones to explore are the Nyuto Onsen, which doubles as a hot spring resort, and the Goshogake Onsen, next to an active volcanic valley.

Lake Tazawa

Lake Tazawa is one of the most beautiful lakes in the Tohoku region. It is famous for being the deepest lake, with a depth of 423 meters. This lake is surrounded by picturesque mountains, creating a breathtaking backdrop.

A boat cruise is one of the best ways to experience the lake and take in the surroundings. The cruise is about 40 minutes long and will give you more history and background about the lake as well as the Tatsuko Statue, a gold statue of a girl believed to have come to this lake to pray she would be able to remain beautiful forever. Legend has it that she was cursed instead, turned into a dragon, and sunk to the bottom of the lake. If you want to take one of the sightseeing boat cruises, they operate between late April and early November and are ¥1200 for adults and ¥600 for children.

If you want to swim in the lake, you can swim between spring and fall on the eastern shore. There are also opportunities to rent pedal boats or paddle boards.

Sendai

Sendai is the largest city in the Tohoku region and has a perfect blend of history and modernity to explore. This city is renowned for its historical sites, including the Zuihoden Mausoleum, the final resting place of the powerful feudal lord Date Masamune, and the ruins of the Aoba Castle, also from Masamune's time. There is a museum on the site of Aoba Castle where you can immerse yourself in the powerful feudal lord's life and what the castle once looked like.

Sendai is also famous for its culinary specialty, *gyutan* (grilled beef tongue), which can be enjoyed at numerous eateries throughout the city. This culinary delight began in 1948 and has been a popular menu item ever since. The most common side dishes with gyutan are oxtail soup or a rice bowl.

Oga Peninsula

The Oga Peninsula is a rugged and scenic coastal area famous for its natural beauty and cultural heritage. Jutting out into the Sea of Japan, the peninsula has many fishing villages, dramatic cliffs, beautiful beaches, and expansive ocean vistas. There are plenty of opportunities to explore the landscape through hiking trails, driving along the coast, and stopping to take in the sights at scenic overlooks. Additionally, this area is rich in cultural traditions, most notably the Namahage. The Namahage is a folklore celebrated annually on New Year's Eve, where men will dress in demon-like costumes and visit homes to ward off evil spirits and bring good fortune for the coming year; the Namahage Museum is worth visiting if you want to learn more about this interesting tradition. With so much to do and see in this part of the Akita Prefecture, visiting the Oga Peninsula will allow you to glimpse into other Japanese traditions while exploring the rugged coastline and taking in breathtaking landscapes.

Sake Brewery Tours

As sake is a traditional Japanese alcoholic beverage, chances are you'll try it at least once while on your trip. However, the Tohoku region is well-known for its processes in creating this iconic beverage, so it is worth going to any of these breweries to tour and taste sake: Hachinohe Shuzo in Aomori, Nanbu Bijin in Iwate, Sake Brewery Hideyoshi in Akita, Otokoyama Honten in Miyagi, Toko Brewery in Yamagata, Daishichi Brewery in Fukushima.

What Events to Enjoy in the Tohoku Region

Soma Nomaoi

The Soma Nomaoi Festival is a traditional equestrian event held annually in Fukushima. It is one of the oldest festivals, dating back a thousand years. It includes various events, including horseback races, a parade with participants dressed in samurai armor riding horses down the street, and a flag-catching competition. This festival typically takes place in May, and it is exciting to attend and immerse yourself in the samurai heritage of Japan.

Where to Eat in the Tohoku Region

Bisai Dining Yuda

Address: 2-2-18 Chuo, Tagajo-shi, Miyagi 985-0873

Hours of operation

- Lunch: 11:30 a.m. to 2 p.m. (last order is at 1:30 p.m.)
- Dinner: 5 p.m. to 11 p.m. (last order is at 10:30 p.m.)

At Bisai Dining Yuda, you can expect a diverse range of cuisine with French, Italian, and Japanese dishes. One of the main and popular dishes this establishment makes is cold pasta with cold tomato sauce, mozzarella, and basil, a flavorful combination perfect for hot summer days. There is also a focus on fish-based dishes made with fresh fish from the Hokkaido and Kyushu regions. You can expect meals to be budget-friendly, with dinner prices around ¥3500.

Oshokujidokoro Osanai

Address: 1–17 1F, 1 Chome Shinmachi, Aomori 030-0801

Hours of operation: 8 a.m. to 2 p.m. and 4 p.m. to 8 p.m. daily

Oshokujidokoro Osanai is a tremendous, budget-friendly restaurant offering hearty and authentic Japanese cuisine highlighting Aomori's culinary traditions. Scallops are some of the top menu options for people who have eaten here, as is their spin on a miso soup called Kenoshiru, which contains cod. Many people love this restaurant for its relaxed atmosphere and generous servings.

Gyoza Yamame

Address: 5-23 Wasecho, Fukushima 960-8044

Hours of operation: 5:30 to 9:30 p.m. daily

Gyoza Yamame is the place to go for gyoza dumplings in Fukushima. This lovely eatery also serves great dumplings and seafood dishes. The restaurant has a laid-back atmosphere that creates a comfortable dining experience.

Kura-Zushi

Address: 1-1-19 Barajima, Akita 010-0065

Hours of operation: 11 a.m. to 11 p.m. daily

Kura-Zushi is another conveyor belt sushi restaurant, which always adds to the fun of eating sushi. Eating sushi this way allows you to pick and choose what you want and enjoy various sushi options. It's pretty cheap per plate (around ¥150), which makes an affordable meal while indulging in this traditional Japanese cuisine.

Yamagyu

Address: 1 Chome-8-15 Yamagata 990-0047

Hours of operation: 11:30 a.m. to 2:30 p.m. and 5:30 p.m. to 9:30 p.m. (closed Tuesdays)

Yamagyu is a minimalist restaurant specializing in premium wagyu beef sourced from local farms and other high-quality ingredients. At this establishment, you can enjoy food from their a la carte menu or a 13-course meal, which is a little more expensive but offers a lot of food for a great price.

What to Eat in the Tohoku Region

Kiritanpo Nabe

Kiritanpo nabe is a hearty hotpot dish that originated in Akita Prefecture. It features grilled rice sticks (kiritanpo) simmered in a flavorful broth with chicken, vegetables, and mushrooms. The rice sticks absorb the delicious broth, resulting in a comforting and satisfying meal.

Hittsumi

Hittsumi is a traditional dumpling soup from Yamagata Prefecture. The dumplings are made from a mixture of flour and water, rolled into small balls, and boiled in a savory broth with vegetables and chicken or pork. Hittsumi is a warming and nourishing dish that's perfect for cold winter days.

Wanko Soba

Wanko soba is a fun and interactive dining experience popular in Iwate Prefecture. It consists of small servings of soba noodles served in tiny bowls (wan), allowing diners to eat as many bowls as they like. Diners can customize their soba with various toppings and condiments, making each bite a unique flavor experience.

Ika Meshi

Ika meshi is a specialty dish from Miyagi Prefecture made with squid stuffed with seasoned rice. The squid is stuffed with a mixture of rice, vegetables, and seasonings and then simmered in a savory broth until tender. Ika meshi is a flavorful and satisfying dish that showcases the region's abundant seafood.

Where to Stay in the Tohoku Region

Hoshino Resorts Aomoriya

Address: 56 Furumakiyama, Misawa, Aomori Prefecture 033-8688

Hoshino Resorts Aomoriya is a perfect retreat in the town of Aomoriya. This traditional ryokan has a resort feel, with hot spring baths that guests enjoy soaking in while taking in the panoramic views of the surrounding landscape. The rooms are also very calm at this ryokan, some with exciting murals and others with a more minimalist Japanese style. Choosing to stay at Hoshino Resorts Aomoriya, even for the night, will guarantee a day and evening of relaxation.

Hotel Metropolitan Morioka New Wing

Address: 2-27 Morioka Ekimaekitadori, Morioka, Iwate Prefecture 020-0033

The Hotel Metropolitan Morioka New Wing is a budget-friendly accommodation with great relaxing rooms, especially as each room has a fireplace. This hotel also has on-site dining options, serving Japanese and international cuisine, and a massage parlor. They also offer bike rental services so you can easily explore the area.

Sendai Royal Park Hotel

Address: 6-2-1 Teraoka, Izumi-ku, Sendai 981-3204

Sendai Royal Park Hotel is a luxury hotel in Sendai that offers many activities that provide maximum comfort and rejuvenation. The elegant rooms feature a European style with warm colors and large windows giving fantastic views of the surrounding area. It is also near the Sendai Izumi Premium Outlet if you want to shop. Yoga sessions are offered in their garden for activities at the hotel. You can also rent bikes to explore the area. This hotel also has several restaurants on-site that serve various cuisines. They also offer free Wi-Fi throughout the hotel.

Hotel Crown Hills Yamagata

Address: 1 Chome-10-1 Kasumichō, Yamagata 990-0039

Hotel Crown Hills Yamagata is a three-star hotel offering comfort for those seeking a more budget-friendly option. The rooms have amenities, including a fridge and kettle, for a pleasant stay. It is also near the Yamagata Station, which makes this hotel an ideal base for exploring the surrounding Tohoku Region, including Fukushima.

Hotel Towadaso

Address: Towadakohanyasumiya-340 Okuse, Towada, Aomori 018-5501

Hotel Towadaso is a three-star hotel with views of Lake Towada, offering a tranquil retreat after a day of exploring. This hotel offers traditional Japanese-style rooms with futons, a low table, and modern amenities, including free Wi-Fi. Guests are welcome to relax in the hot spring bath with a rotational schedule for men and women.

What Not to Do in the Tohoku Region

Don't Visit Off-Limit Areas in Fukushima

Since the 2011 earthquake caused significant destruction in Fukushima and the Fukushima Daiichi Nuclear Power Station complex, much of the area has remained off-limits. Decontamination efforts have been made, and much of the radiation has been eradicated. However, if you come across any off-limit regions, don't trespass into them, as these posted warnings are there for your safety.

Follow Onsen Etiquette at Akiu Onsen

Familiarize yourself with onsen etiquette before visiting Akiu Onsen. This includes washing thoroughly before entering the hot springs, refraining from bringing towels into the water and avoiding loud behavior or horseplay. Some onsen facilities in Akiu Onsen may have specific dress codes or requirements for bathing attire. Follow these guidelines to avoid any discomfort or embarrassment during your visit. Many onsen establishments in Akiu Onsen prohibit the use of electronic devices such as smartphones, cameras, or tablets in the bathing areas. Respect these rules to maintain the privacy and comfort of other guests.

Don't Ignore Trail Marker at Oirase Gorge

Oirase Gorge has well-marked hiking trails, but it's essential to pay attention to trail markers and signage to avoid getting lost or straying off the designated paths. Weather conditions in Oirase Gorge can change rapidly, especially in mountainous areas. Check the weather forecast before your visit and be prepared for changes in temperature, rainfall, or other weather-related factors. While the gorge has some beautiful waterfalls and streams, swimming may be prohibited in certain areas due to safety concerns or environmental protection. Respect any signage or warnings regarding swimming restrictions. Be prepared for your hike by bringing essential items such as water, snacks, sunscreen, insect repellent, a map or GPS device, and appropriate clothing and footwear for hiking in varying terrain and weather conditions.

Next Stop: Sapporo and the Hokkaido Region

Despite some of the hardships Tohoku faced, especially with the devastating 2011 earthquake, this beautiful northeastern region of Japan is bursting with many things to see, do, experience, and taste—especially with their greenhouses boasting delicious fruit throughout the year. In this chapter, we explored some of the historical parts of Tohoku to visit, including the renowned Hirosaki Castle and surrounding parklands, so that you can immerse yourself in Japanese history while taking in the sights of the cherry blossom trees. Additionally, as this part of Japan has plenty of outdoor activities, you will find plenty of ways to take in the thrills of outdoor adventuring and find new perspectives on Japan.

We will travel to Sapporo and Hokkaido next, where there is more to see and do in Japan. Sapporo is known for its beer, while Hokkaido offers more outdoor adventures, especially in the winter.

Chapter 8:

Sapporo and The Hokkaido Region—Dos and Don'ts

Sapporo's name traces back to the Ainu language, a native language of the aboriginal Ainu people who lived in the Hokkaido region long before the real settlement began in the city in the late 1860s. In Ainu, Sapporo, or "sat poro pet," is said to translate to "dry great river." The name's significance refers to the Toyohira River, which flows through Sapporo, an iconic landmark where you can see salmon swimming upstream. It's also a place that offers a serene atmosphere away from the hustle and bustle of Sapporo.

Discovering the Hokkaido Region

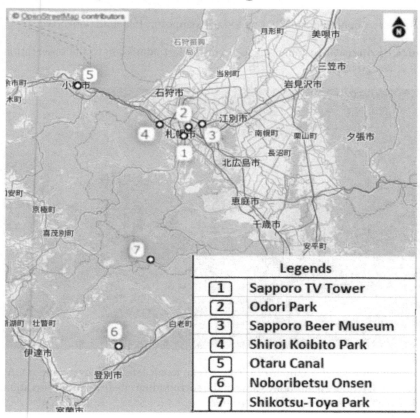

	Legends
1	Sapporo TV Tower
2	Odori Park
3	Sapporo Beer Museum
4	Shiroi Koibito Park
5	Otaru Canal
6	Noboribetsu Onsen
7	Shikotsu-Toya Park

The Hokkaido Region is Japan's northernmost island, with some of the most diverse landscapes to explore. This region is surrounded by the Sea of Japan, the Sea of Okhotsk, and the Pacific Ocean, allowing you to explore rugged coastlines, picturesque mountains, and expansive fields. As Hokkaido is in the north, you can expect that the seasons will allow for a wide range of activities, from hiking and enjoying outdoor festivals to enjoying plenty of winter activities.

What is most interesting is that this part of Japan, specifically Sapporo, did not grow until 1869. Until then, the Hokkaido Region was the home of the Ainu people. While much of the Ainu people have long been assimilated, some have kept to their family's roots and live mainly in the northern parts of Hokkaido. There is much to see and do in the Hokkaido Region, especially in Sapporo, so let's get into it.

What to Do in the Hokkaido Region

Sapporo TV Tower

Address: 1 Chome Odorinishi, Chuo Ward, Sapporo, Hokkaido 060-0042

Hours of operation: 9 a.m. to 10 p.m. (the last admission to the observation deck is at 9:30 p.m.)

Completed in 1957, the Sapporo TV Tower is an iconic landmark over Sapporo. At 483 feet tall, it offers panoramic views of the surrounding city from the observation deck, which is 90 meters above the ground.

In addition to going to the observation deck, the tower has three lower floors with shops and restaurants. You can also access Aurora Town from the underground shopping street in the tower's basement.

Tickets for the observation deck can be purchased on the tower's third level. There are two options: One allows you in at the time of purchase, and the other allows you to enter the observation deck during the day and then return at night to take in the night scenery of Sapporo.

Ticket type	Observation entrance fee	Day/night tickets
Adults and high school students	¥1000	¥1500
Elementary school and junior high school students	¥500	¥700

Ōdori Park

Ōdori Park is an expansive green space in the heart of Sapporo, spanning about 20 blocks from east to west. This park was established in 1871 to differentiate the north administrative side of Sapporo from the south residential and commercial area. Today, the park is a tranquil oasis lined with trees, flowerbeds, sculptures, and fountains. This park is also home to various events and festivals, including the Sapporo Summer and Snow Festivals.

Sapporo Beer Museum

Address: 9 Chome-1-1 Kita 7 Jōhigashi, Higashi Ward, Hokkaido 065-8633

Hours of operation: 11 a.m. to 6 p.m. (The last admission is at 5:30 p.m., and the museum is closed on Mondays.)

Did you know that Hokkaido is the birthplace of Japanese beer? Sapporo beer is the oldest beer in Japan and still a popular option among beer drinkers. At the Sapporo Beer Museum, you can explore exhibits that detail the history of beer production in Japan and how Sapporo was influential in Japan's brewing industry. This museum will also give you a glimpse into the brewing techniques, vintage advertisements, and a collection of brewing equipment. If you want to enhance your experience, a guided tour is available where you will get to watch a film about Sapporo's history and finish the tour with a tasting of Sapporo Beer Kuro Label, one of the original brews. This attraction is free unless you want to take a guided tour, which is ¥500 per person. Patrons wishing to taste beer must be at least 20 years old.

Shiroi Koibito Park

Address: 2 Chome-11-36 Miyanosawa 2 Jo, Nishi Ward, Sapporo, Hokkaido 063-0052

Hours of operation: 10 a.m. to 5 p.m. daily (the last admission is at 4 p.m.)

If you have a sweet tooth, you will want to check out Shiroi Koibito Park. Established by Ishiya, a renowned cookie company, this park offers a glimpse into the production process of their signature Shiroi Koibito, a white chocolate cookie sandwich. At this attraction, there is a free area where you can buy some sweets to take home or enjoy some matcha or lunch at the restaurant. If you want to go behind the scenes, you can pay for a self-guided factory tour to explore different chocolate-related exhibits and watch the cookies being made. The self-guided tour is ¥600 per person.

Otaru Canal

The Otaru Canal in Otaru is a historic waterway that was a central hub for transporting goods up to the early 20th century. At the time, the Otaru Canal was significant in supporting the city's economic development, especially with the smaller ships transporting goods from larger ships into the area. When modern dock facilities were implemented, the canal was no longer needed. It fell into disarray until the 1980s when a group of locals banded together to revive it. Today, the Otaru Canal is a lovely place to stroll and admire the preserved warehouses and stone-built buildings that have been converted into shops. The canal also serves as a place for the Otaru Snow Light Festival in February.

Noboribetsu Onsen

Noboribetsu Onsen in Noboribetsu is one of Japan's most famous hot spring resorts for its therapeutic waters and stunning natural surroundings. There are 11 types of thermal waters in this hot spring resort, all of which are believed to possess various healing properties. You can immerse yourself in the baths, which range from outdoor to indoor and are infused with different minerals. Once you're done, it is worth exploring the spa town and the surrounding area where you can explore Jigokudani, where the resort town gets its hot spring waters. Autumn is one of the best times to explore Jigokudani due to the valley's vibrant red, orange, and yellow hues.

Shikotsu-Toya National Park

Shikotsu-Toya National Park is a great place to go if you're an outdoor enthusiast. This national park encompasses the scenic Lake Shikotsu and Lake Toya and surrounding volcanic landscapes, hot springs, and dense forests. Boating and sightseeing cruises are popular at the park, especially along Lake Toya, where you can take in the sights of the Mount Usu volcano. While it hasn't erupted since 2000, it is still considered to be active. To get closer to the volcano's summit, take the Usuzan Ropeway, which runs between 9 a.m. and 4 p.m. daily.

Usuzan Ropeway Tickets

Ticket type	Price
Adult	¥1800
Child	¥900

Winter Sports in Hokkaido

Given how far north Hokkaido is, it is easily a haven for those who love to participate in winter activities, including skiing, dog sledding, snowshoeing, winter rafting, and snowmobiling.

What Events to Enjoy in the Hokkaido Region

Sapporo Summer Festival

The Sapporo Summer Festival is an annual event that typically takes place in late July to early August in Ōdori Park. The main highlight of this event is the beer garden, where attendees can enjoy local and internal brews and food from various vendors. The venue is split into multiple sections based on where the beer and food are coming from. For example, Germany has its own "village" and so on. This festival is free to attend.

Sapporo Snow Festival

The Sapporo Snow Festival is a fun winter event that began in the 1950s when high school students created six snow sculptures in Ōdori Park. Since then, the event has expanded and brings millions of people together every February to admire the huge snow and ice sculptures around the Ōdori, Susukino, and Tsu Dome Sites. These beautiful sculptures are also lit up from sundown until about 10 p.m. each night.

In addition to admiring the beautiful sculptures, you can immerse yourself in outdoor winter activities and enjoy food from local vendors. If you plan to attend this event, it is ¥1500 for a ticket and allows you a full day at the festival.

Furano Lavender Festival

The Furano Lavender Festival celebrates the iconic lavender fields in the Hokkaido region, spanning various locations, including Farm Tomita and Flower Land Kamifurano. This festival allows you to immerse yourself in the stunning vistas of blooming lavender. In addition to taking many Instagram-worthy photos of the vibrant purple fields, you can enjoy many other flowers in the area, including poppies, lupins, and sunflowers.

If you intend to experience this festival, getting to all the fields without transportation can be challenging. There are sightseeing buses if you do not want to rent a car for your trip.

Asahikawa Winter Festival

The Asahikawa Winter Festival is similar to the Sapporo Winter Festival and takes place around the same time in February at Asahibashi. At this festival, you can admire an impressive display of snow and ice sculptures, ranging from iconic landmarks to mythical creatures, between the Asahibashi site and Heiwa Dori. In addition to admiring the impressive sculptures, you can watch a fireworks show, enjoy food from local vendors, and watch people create ice sculptures.

Otaru Snow Light Path Festival

The Otaru Snow Light Path Festival is an enchanting event in which Otaru's canal and historic streets are adorned with thousands of snow lanterns and light installations, creating a beautiful and magical atmosphere. This festival takes place around the same time as the Sapporo and Asahikawa Winter Festivals, making it possible for all three of them to attend. If you want to be a part of this festival, there are volunteer opportunities where you can make snow lanterns with the locals, which is always a fun experience for all ages.

Where to Eat in the Hokkaido Region

Moliere

Address: Lafayette Miyagaoka 1F, 2-1-1 Miyagaoka, Chuo-ku, Sapporo, Hokkaido 064-0959

Hours of operation: 11 a.m. to 2 p.m. and 5:30 p.m. to 8 p.m. daily

Moliere is a three-Michelin-starred restaurant in the heart of Sapporo, serving delicious French dishes. The chef at this restaurant is trained in France and showcases his expertise in every dish created using fresh, local ingredients. Many who have eaten at Moliere loved the Japanese twist on the dishes and the atmosphere.

Sushidokoro Kihara

Address: 2-1-2, Yunokawa-cho, Hakodate, Hokkaido 142-0932

Hours of operation: 11:30 a.m. to 10 p.m. The last order is at 9 p.m. The restaurant is closed on Wednesdays and national holidays.

Sushidokoro Kihara is one of the best places to get sushi in Hokkaido. Using the freshest ingredients and fish from the chef's hometown, you will feast on expertly prepared sushi rolls that are flavorful with each bite.

Hakodate Asaichi Aji no Ichiban

Address: 11-13 Wakamatsucho, Hakodate, Hokkaido 040-0063

Hours of operation: 7 a.m. to 3 p.m. daily

If you're looking for a place to grab breakfast or lunch, Hakodate Asaichi Aji no Ichiban in the bustling Hakodate Morning Market is worth visiting. Given the restaurant's location close to the water, if you order meals with fish or seafood, you can expect the freshest as they would have been caught that morning. Even if you're not up for fish or seafood, you can enjoy a range of other dishes on the menu, including ramen and donburi (rice-based meals).

Soup Curry Shabazo

Address: B1F, Sapporo North Plaza Building, Kita 1-jo Nishi 4-chome, Chuo-ku, Sapporo, Hokkaido

Hours of operation: 11:30 a.m. to 3 p.m. and 5 p.m. to 10 p.m. (closed Sundays). The lunch and dinner times will end if the restaurant sells out of soup.

If you love soup and curry, definitely check out Soup Curry Shabazo. At this establishment, you can enjoy soup curry with a wide range of options, including chicken, beef, lamb, fish, and seafood tailored to your liking with spiciness. You can expect a hearty meal that will leave you feeling full and satisfied.

Yakitori no Ippei

Address: 1-17-3 Nakajima-cho , Muroran-shi, Hokkaido 050-0074

Hours of operation

- Monday to Thursday: 5 p.m. to 11 p.m.
- Friday and Saturday: 5 p.m. to 12 a.m.
- Sunday: 5 p.m. to 10 p.m.

Yakitori no Ippei is renowned for its yakitori, which is grilled meat on a skewer. There is a wide variety of options, including chicken and pork, which pair well with the delicious dipping sauce made from mustard and egg yolks. Prices are low here, making it a great place to eat dinner.

What to Eat in the Hokkaido Region

Genghis Khan (Jingisukan)

Genghis Khan is a popular grilled lamb dish that originated in Hokkaido. Thinly sliced lamb is marinated in a savory sauce and grilled over a charcoal barbecue. The meat is typically served with vegetables and dipped in a tangy sauce, making it a flavorful and satisfying meal.

Soup Curry

Soup curry is a unique Hokkaido specialty that combines Japanese curry with a light and fragrant soup broth. The curry is often loaded with vegetables and meat or seafood, creating a hearty and nourishing dish. Each restaurant has its own variations and spice levels, so you can customize your soup curry to suit your taste.

Hokkaido Ramen

Hokkaido is famous for its delicious ramen noodles, which are characterized by their rich and creamy broth made from pork bones (tonkotsu) or miso. Hokkaido ramen is typically topped with ingredients like roasted pork (chashu), buttered corn, and green onions, creating a comforting and flavorful bowl of noodles.

Sapporo Beer and Jingisukan Pairing

Sapporo is home to one of Japan's oldest and most famous breweries, and no visit to the city would be complete without trying Sapporo Beer. Pair your beer with a delicious serving of Genghis Khan (Jingisukan) for the ultimate Hokkaido dining experience. The refreshing beer complements the savory grilled lamb perfectly, making it a popular combination among locals and visitors alike.

Sapporo Snow Crab (Zuwai-gani)

Hokkaido is renowned for its succulent snow crab, which is harvested from the cold waters of the Sea of Japan. Sapporo snow crab is prized for its sweet and delicate flavor, and it's often served in a variety of dishes such as grilled crab legs, sushi, sashimi, and hotpot (kani nabe).

Where to Stay in the Hokkaido Region

Nest Hotel Sapporo Ekimae

Address: 2 Chome-9 Kita 2 Jonishi, Chuo Ward, Sapporo, Hokkaido 060-0002

Nest Hotel Sapporo Ekimae is an excellent option for budget-friendly accommodation. This hotel has basic rooms with modern amenities to make your stay comfortable and relaxing. It's also right by Sapporo station, which makes it an excellent hub for exploring Sapporo's attractions.

Hotel Neu Schloss Otaru

Address: 3 Chome-282 Shukutsu, Otaru, Hokkaido 047-0047

Hotel Neu Schloss Otaru offers comfortable accommodations in simple rooms decorated in a European style. This hotel is in a convenient location, making it easy for you to explore the historic canal area, among other attractions in Otaru. Some rooms have great ocean views, as does the private open bath.

Hotel Nord Otaru

Address: 1 Chome-4-16 Ironai, Otaru, Hokkaido 047-0031

Hotel Nord Otaru is a four-star hotel situated along the historic Otaru Canal. All of the rooms are bright and spacious, offering a comfortable stay. Some rooms have great views of the river and the mountains in the distance. Free Wi-Fi is also available throughout the property.

Sapporo Grand Hotel

Address: 4 Chome Kita 1 Jonishi, Chuo Ward, Sapporo, Hokkaido 060-0001

The Sapporo Grand Hotel is as grand as it sounds. This five-star hotel has a shopping center, seven dining options, and free Wi-Fi throughout the property. Additionally, it is close to transportation hubs, making it easy to travel to Sapporo's various attractions. If you want to indulge in a bit of self-care, be sure to book a massage or beauty treatment in its wellness center.

Keio Plaza Hotel Sapporo

Address: 2-1, North 5 West 7, Chuo-ku, Sapporo, Hokkaido 060-0005
If you're looking for another luxury stay, Keio Plaza Hotel Sapporo is another excellent choice due to its convenience, comfort, and amenities. This hotel is near Sapporo station, which is helpful for traveling around the city to various attractions, including the Sapporo Beer Museum. Additionally, the rooms are spacious to provide maximum comfort for unwinding after a day of exploring. There are also massages available, as well as a sauna.

What Not to Do in the Hokkaido Region

Don't Expect Heavily Salted Roads

The Hokkaido Region sees the most snow in the winter and they don't use a lot of salt to melt the snow and ice, making it a slippery walk. If you don't have good, treaded boots for the snow, pick up some spikes for your shoes to prevent you from slipping and sliding everywhere.

Don't Forget the Underground Walkways

If the weather is cold and snowy, use the underground walkways while you're in Sapporo. Your toes will thank you!

Don't Take the Train to Hokkaido

Given how far north the Hokkaido region is, taking the train is the slowest way to get there, as bullet trains are not yet servicing this part of Japan. If you plan to go to the Hokkaido region, take a domestic flight.

Next Stop: The Shikoku Region

Sapporo and the Hokkaido Region is another significant region to visit, especially if you love being outdoors and immersing yourself in outdoor activities like skiing. In this part of Japan, you learned about the many attractions that make Sapporo and the Hokkaido Region unique, especially with the stunning rolling hills in Furano and Biei and the famous beer at the Sapporo Beer Museum. With the tips you have learned in this chapter, you can make a fantastic itinerary for this Japanese region to further immerse yourself in their culture and history.

In the next chapter, we will venture to the Shikoku Region, renowned for its tranquil atmosphere and pilgrimage history. Many people forget about this region, but there are many places to visit that will enhance their appreciation for this beautiful country.

Chapter 9:

The Shikoku Region—Dos and Don'ts

T he Shikoku Region in Japan earned its name after the island it encompasses. This island is the smallest of Japan's four main islands in the archipelago, and its name, Shikoku, translates to "four provinces." The four former provinces that once made up the island were Awa, Tosa, Sanuki, and Iyo. As the country grew and became more unified over the centuries, these four areas transitioned into the modern prefectures of Tokushima, Kōchi, Kagawa, and Ehime.

Discover the Shikoku Region

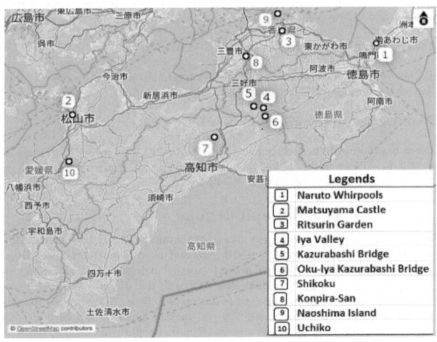

The Shikoku region is in the southwest of Japan and is one of the most tranquil main islands to visit, thanks to its beautiful natural landscape. Each prefecture has many unique attractions to explore. In Tokushima, famed for its Awa Odori Festival and Awa Kamogawa Fireworks, you'll find many stunning valleys and the picturesque whirlpools of the Naruto Strait. Kōchi is the largest prefecture, boasting a rugged coastline and beautiful beaches that make you feel like you have stepped off the grid. Kagawa, nicknamed the "Udon Prefecture," is celebrated for its delicious thick noodles; this prefecture is also where you will find the iconic Ritsurin Garden. Finally, Ehime is renowned for its serene countryside and historic sites, including Dogo Onsen and Matsuyama Castle.

No matter what type of traveler you are, whether you are outdoorsy and seeking to explore and take in the sea views, mountains, and rivers to immerse yourself in the pilgrimage history of Shikoku or learn about the historical significance of Matsuyama castle, this part of Japan is not short of experiences to immerse yourself in.

What to Do in the Shikoku Region

Naruto Whirlpools

The Naruto whirlpools are some of the most extraordinary natural phenomena in the world. These whirlpools found along the Naruto Strait between Awaji Island and Shikoku Island are caused by the complex interaction of the tidal currents, ocean currents, and the shape of the underwater topography. As the tidal currents flow, they encounter changes in water depth and experience the coastline's irregularities, creating the whirlpool effect. The whirlpools can be as large as 20 meters in diameter, depending on the tide and season conditions. Naturally, because of how neat the whirlpools are, they bring tourists to marvel at their impressive natural beauty.

If you want to see the Naruto whirlpools, there are a couple of ways to do this: by boat or on the Akashi Kaikyo Bridge. On the Ōge Island end, there is a small corridor called Uzu no Michi. This corridor is beneath the bridge, which allows visitors to walk out over the ocean and watch the whirlpools through the glass floor. This corridor also has floor-to-ceiling windows to take total views of the Strait.

If you want to get up close and personal, a tourist boat ride on the Aqua Eddy or Wonder Naruto is the way to go. The same company runs the boats; however, Wonder Naruto has an upper deck and an additional cost. If you go on the smaller Aqua Eddy, you must book a reservation, as the boat only holds 46 people. What is cool about taking the Aqua Eddy is that the ship has an observatory room that allows you to see up to one meter below sea level and the whirlpools swirling underwater instead of marveling at them from above!

Best Time to See the Naruto Whirlpools

The best times to see the whirlpools will vary depending on the time of day and year. For example, they will be more visible between 1 and 2 p.m. in the spring. If you plan on checking out the whirlpools, your best bet is to do a quick Google search. If you are going to take one of the boat trips, the times will be posted with handy emojis to indicate the best times.

Uzu no Michi Corridor
Hours of operation

- March to September: 9 a.m. to 6 p.m. (the last admission is at 5:30 p.m.)
  - April 29 to May 6 (Golden Week): 8 a.m. to 7 p.m. (the last admission is at 6:30 p.m.)
- October to February: 9 a.m. to 5 p.m. (the last admission is at 4:30 p.m.)

Ticket type	Price
Adult	¥510
Junior high/high school students	¥410
Elementary school student	¥260
Children 6 and under	Free

Naruto Wonder and Aqua Eddy
The trips to see the whirlpools up close are around 30 minutes long if you take the boat.

Naruto Wonder

The departure schedule for the Naruto Wonder begins at 9 a.m. and runs 12 trips until 4:20 p.m. You'll need a second ticket to access the observation deck, which can be purchased at the ticket booth.

Ticket type	Main deck	Observation deck (first class cabin)
Adult	¥1800	¥1000
Child (elementary school)	¥900	¥500

Aqua Eddy

Aqua Eddy tickets must be reserved up to four days in advance. This boat's departure schedule begins at 9:15 a.m. and runs 15 daily trips until 4:15 p.m.

Ticket type	Price
Adult	¥2400
Child (elementary school)	¥1200

Matsuyama Castle

Address: 1 Marunouchi, Matsuyama, Ehime 790-0008

Hours of operation

- 9 a.m. to 5 p.m. daily (hours are subject to change based on the season.)
- Ropeway: 8:30 a.m. to 5:30 p.m. daily
    - The ropeway runs until 5 p.m. in December and until 6 p.m. in August.
- Chairlift: 8:30 p.m. to 5 p.m. daily

Matsuyama Castle is one of the original castles left in Japan, and it is still intact. Built between 1602 and 1628 atop Mount Katsuyama, it played a significant role in the region's feudal history when the Tokugawa family reigned; however, their relatives, the Matsudaira family, lived in the castle from 1635 until the end of the feudal era.

When you visit Matsuyama Castle, you can explore the impressive grounds with stone walls, fortified gates, and traditional wooden structures. These give you a glimpse into Japan's medieval architecture and defense strategies. In addition, you can explore the Ninomaru Garden at the base of Matsuyama Castle, which was once the castle's second circle of defense.

Ticket type	Matsuyama Castle	Ninomaru Park	Chairlift and ropeway (one way)	Chair Lift and ropeway (round trip)
Adult	¥520	¥200	¥270	¥520
Child	¥160	¥100	¥140	¥260

Ritsurin Garden

Address: 1 Chome-20-16 Ritsurinchō, Takamatsu, Kagawa 760-0073

Hours of operation: 6:30 a.m. to 6 p.m. daily

The stunning Ritsurin Garden in the Kagawa Prefecture is one of the most exquisite places you can visit. Completed in 1745 after 100 years of construction, this garden served as a private retreat for the Matsudaira family. You can explore this garden's expansive landscape with thirteen hills and six ponds and stroll across one of the many bridges. Additionally, you can enjoy boat rides on the ponds or visit the Kikugetsu-tei Teahouse, where you can enjoy a cup of matcha tea. Ritsurin Garden is also a great place to see in the spring, as the park has over 300 cherry blossoms, which create beautiful reflections in the ponds. This garden also has nightly evening illumination, adding a new enchantment level.

Iya Valley

Iya Valley is in the Tokushima Prefecture and is renowned for its rugged terrain and lush forests. Historically, this valley served as a refuge for the defeated samurai members of the Taira Clan when they lost the Genpei War between 1180 and 1185). Interestingly, many of their descendants still live in tiny villages in the valley.

Visiting Iya Valley is a great place to go for a day of outdoor adventure. Explore the scenic beauty along the various hiking trails, cross iconic vine bridges (Iya Kazurabashi Bridge and the Oku-Iya Kazurabashi Bridges) over the Iya River, visit the restored samurai house that was the Kita clan's residence, and take a sightseeing cruise along the Oboke and Koboke Gorges, which are near the entrance to Iya Valley.

Kazurabashi Bridge

Hours of operation

- April to June: 8 a.m. to 6 p.m. daily
- July to August: 7:30 a.m. to 6:30 p.m. daily
- September to March: 8 a.m. to 5 p.m. daily

Ticket type	Price
Adult	¥550
Children	¥350

Oku-Iya Kazurabashi Bridges

Hours of operation
- April to June and September to November: 9 a.m. to 5 p.m. daily
- July to August: 8 a.m. to 6 p.m. daily

Ticket type	Price
Adults	¥550
Children	¥350

Oboke Sightseeing Boat Cruise
The Oboke Sightseeing Boat Cruise is about 30 minutes long and takes you down the Yoshino River. The first departure leaves at 9 a.m., and the last is at 3:30 p.m.

Ticket type	Price
Adult	¥1500
Children	¥750

Shikoku Pilgrimage

The Shikoku Pilgrimage is one of the most significant areas in the Shikoku Region and is renowned as one of Japan's most spiritual journeys anyone can take. This hike was established over 1,200 years ago and goes by 88 Buddhist temples along the 745-mile trek. These temples are all associated with the Buddhist monk Kobo

Daishi, who founded the Shingon sect of Buddhism. Some 150,000 people embark on this journey yearly, and completing the pilgrimage is a transformative experience that symbolizes the quest for enlightenment, self-discovery, and spiritual purification.

The pilgrimage is a challenging hike. You'll traverse diverse landscapes, from rugged mountains to serene coastal villages, and immerse yourself in Shikoku's cultural heritage and natural beauty. If you do it fully, it takes 45 days to complete the journey on foot (but many break it down into smaller chunks). Even if you do a small bit of the pilgrimage, it will be an experience unlike anything else in Japan.

Konpira-San

Address: 892-1, Kotohira, Nakatado District, Kagawa 766-8501

Hours of operation: Main gate: 6 a.m. to 6 p.m., Main shrine: 7 a.m. to 5 p.m.

Konpira-san (also known as Kotoshira-gu Shrine) is one of the most sacred shrines in Japan. Founded sometime in the first century, the shrine is dedicated to Omonoushi-no-Mikoto (or Knonpira), a maritime god. As such, this shrine has a historical significance to Japan's maritime culture as it has been a place of worship for sailors and fishermen seeking protection while they are at sea.

As a warning: Visiting Konpira-san is a literal stair climber. It is 1,368 steps to the main shrine. However, if you brave the challenging climb, you will be rewarded with great views of the surrounding landscape at the top (and along the way). About halfway (around the 785 steps), you'll find shopping, restaurants, and a museum.

Naoshima Island

If you love admiring different kinds of art, you will want to go to Naoshima Island. This island is well-known for its vibrant art scene and beautiful natural landscape. While visiting, you can explore a variety of contemporary art museums, installations, and outdoor sculptures scattered across the island. Highlights of the art galleries worth exploring include the Benesse House Museum, which features a collection of modern artworks and doubles as a resort, and the Chichu Art Museum, a primarily underground gallery showcasing an immersive art experience.

To reach Naoshima Island, you will need to take a ferry. Ferries can be caught from the Takamatsu Port in Kagawa and Uno Port in Okayama, bringing you to Miyanoura Port (west side) or Honmura Port (east side) on Naoshima.

Uchiko

Uchiko is a historical town in the Ehime Prefecture. This town flourished during the Edo period as a center for producing wax and paper. Visiting this town will give you a glimpse into its past, allowing you to admire the well-preserved merchant houses, warehouses, and streetscapes. One of the highlights of exploring the rich history of this village is visiting the Kamihaga Residence, which will give you an in-depth look at the wax-making industry. Another highlight is the Uchiko-za Theater, a theater built in 1916 and famous for its dramatic performances thanks to the trapdoors and hidden passageways.

What Events to Enjoy in the Shikoku Region

Awa Odori Festival

The Awa Odori Festival is an annual event during the Obon season in mid-August in the Tokushima Prefecture. It is believed to have originated 400 years ago, though its purpose has a few theories. Some say this traditional dance is connected to conventional Bon-odori dancing. Others think the dance was created to celebrate the completion of Tokushima Castle in 1587. Some even believe this dance is rooted in the fury dance.

Whatever the theory is, this significant cultural event has transformed into one of the largest dance festivals in Japan, attracting thousands of people from across the country and around the world. Participants in the event are a combination of professional and amateur dancers who dress in vibrant costumes as they parade through the streets, dancing to rhythmic drumming, flutes, and other traditional instruments in synchronized formations. Everyone is welcome to attend and watch, and if you want to participate, you can register with the Niwaka Ren, who will teach you the dance steps. This is an iconic event you won't want to miss!

Where to Eat in the Shikoku Region

Honetsukidori Ikkaku Takamatsu

Address: 4-11 Kajiyamachi, Takamatsu, Kagawa 760-0028

Hours of operation: Monday to Friday: 11 a.m. to 2 p.m. and 5 p.m. to 10 p.m., Saturday and Sunday: 11 a.m. to 10 p.m.

Honetsukidori Ikkaku Takamatsu is a popular dining option among locals in Takamatsu. It is famous for its spicy chicken on the bone. This restaurant uses a special oven that spices and cooks the chicken to make this dish. The menu has more to discover, including delicious rice sides and salad options. The wait time can be lengthy, but restaurant patrons say it is worth the wait, and the prices are cheap!

Dogo-no Machiya

Address: 14-26 Dogoyunomachi, Matsuyama, Ehime 790-0842

Hours of operation: 10 a.m. to 10 p.m. daily

If you are craving a burger while on your journey through the Ehime Prefecture, Dogo-no Machiya is the place to go! This establishment offers different burgers and sandwiches along with different kinds of sides. Many people also love the atmosphere of Dogo-no Machiya, which has one area overlooking a garden. Prices are relatively low for the food, especially if you eat here for lunch.

Cin Na Mon

Address: 2310-31 Miyaura, Naoshima, Kagawa District, Kagawa 761-3110

Hours of operation: 11 a.m. to 3 p.m. and 5 p.m. to 10 p.m. daily

Cin Na Mon is a chic restaurant near the Miyanoura Port, where you can experience a unique dining atmosphere in their tatami-fitted rooms. At this establishment, you can expect plenty of delicious seafood dishes made with freshly caught fish, including fried chicken and sashimi, among other Japanese delicacies.

Udon Honjin Yamadaya

Address: 3186 Murecho Mure, Takamatsu, Kagawa 761-0121

Hours of operation: 10 a.m. to 8 p.m. daily

Did you know that Kagawa is nicknamed "Udon Noodle Prefecture?" Due to the geography of Kagama, it's not an ideal base to grow rice, but wheat thrives here! Thus, the grain is used to make the delicious, thick, chewy noodles in many of the region's staple dishes. To taste these classic noodles, you will want to eat at Udon Honjin Yamadaya, one of the best places to enjoy udon noodle dishes. This eatery serves udon noodles with many options, including soups and tempura.

Tsukasa Kochihonten

Address: 1-2-15 Harimayacho, Kochi City, Kochi Prefecture 780-0822

Hours of operation: Monday to Saturday: 11:30 a.m. to 10 p.m., Sunday: 11 a.m. to 9 p.m.

If you want to dine on traditional Japanese dishes, visit Tsukasa Kochihonten. This establishment offers a range of menu options, many of which are seafood-based, in a beautifully appointed space. You can expect high-quality ingredients and friendly staff that accommodate those with food allergies.

What to Eat in the Shikoku Region

Sanuki Udon

Sanuki Udon is a type of thick wheat noodle that originated in Kagawa Prefecture and is known for its chewy texture and ability to absorb the flavors of the broth. Enjoyed both hot and cold, Sanuki Udon is typically served in a savory broth with toppings such as green onions, tempura, or kamaboko (fish cake).

Tai Meshi

Tai Meshi, or sea bream rice, is a specialty dish of Kochi Prefecture. It features tender sea bream fillets grilled or simmered in a soy-based sauce and served over a bed of steamed rice. The delicate flavor of the seabream pairs perfectly with the fragrant rice, creating a simple yet satisfying meal.

Katsuo no Tataki

Katsuo no Tataki is a dish made from lightly seared bonito (skipjack tuna) that is sliced thinly and served with grated ginger, garlic, and soy sauce. The bonito is briefly seared over high heat to create a smoky flavor while maintaining its tender texture. Katsuo no Tataki is a popular dish in Kochi Prefecture, where fresh bonito is abundant.

Jakoten

Jakoten is a type of fried fish cake made from pureed fish paste mixed with flour and seasoning, then deep-fried until crispy. It is a specialty of Ehime Prefecture and is often served as a snack or side dish. Jakoten can be enjoyed on its own or dipped in soy sauce or a tangy ponzu sauce.

Where to Stay in the Shikoku Region

Iya Bijin

Address: 9-3 Nishiiyayamamura Zentoku, Miyoshi, Tokushima 778-0102

Iya Bijin is a simple inn in Tokushima offering a unique blend of traditional charm and modern comfort. This inn is set against a backdrop of valleys and winding rivers, allowing you to find tranquility and relaxation during your stay. All rooms have tatami flooring and shoji screens to encompass traditional Japanese aesthetics. Additionally, this ryokan offers an inclusive meal package for dinner and breakfast at the on-site restaurant.

Sunriver Oboke

Address: 1259-1 Nishiu, Yamashiro-cho, Miyoshi City, Tokushima Prefecture 779-5451

Sunriver Oboke is a picturesque accommodation along the Yoshino River, providing a relaxing and serene atmosphere. You will find several room options at this accommodation to suit your needs, including some with a shared bathroom. Additionally, you can enjoy amenities, including a hot spring bath and sauna. They also have free Wi-Fi in the rooms.

The Chelsea Breath

Address: 1878 Kagawacho Kawahigashishimo, Takamatsu 761-1705

The Chelsea Breath is a three-star hotel offering stylish and comfortable accommodations with modern amenities to enhance your stay. The rooms at this hotel all have views of the surrounding garden or mountains, making for a lovely way to wake up each day. The Chelsea Breath is close to the Ritsurin Garden and Takamatsu Castle for attractions nearby.

Tosa Gyoen

Address: 1 Chome-4-8 Ōkawasuji, Kochi 780-0052

Tosa Gyoen is in a convenient location in the heart of Kōchi, with beautiful rooms decorated in the traditional Japanese style (or you can choose Western-styled ones if that is what you prefer). The location of this accommodation is near transportation so you can easily travel to the landmarks in the area. You may also choose to include breakfast with your room fee.

Cosmos Guesthouse

Address: 1861-2, Akano, Tokushima, 779-5452

If you're looking for budget-friendly accommodation in the Shikoku Region, check out the Cosmos Guesthouse. This is a good option if you intend to explore outdoors, as it is situated along the Yoshino River. All rooms are private; however, the bathroom is shared.

What Not to Do in the Shikoku Region

Don't Approach Japanese Pit Vipers

Shikoku's Pilgrimage Trail has plenty of outdoor adventures to do, but be mindful if you come across Japanese pit vipers. These snakes are between 18 and 32 inches in size and are either pale gray, reddish-brown, or yellow-brown, making it easy to camouflage against the vegetation. Be mindful of your surroundings, and if you get a bit, seek help immediately.

Don't Get Stung by Giant Hornets

The hornets in the Shikoku region are giant and very aggressive. These flying insects can grow up to almost two inches long and have bright yellow heads. If you come across a hornet's nest, be wary and stay away from it. If you get stung, you'll need medical care as soon as possible, as their venom can impact your nervous system.

Next Stop: Kyushu and Okinawa

The tranquility and pilgrimage history of the Shikoku Region will turn over a new leaf as you discover this hidden gem of Japan. This chapter has given you plenty of ways to explore the region, including the historical town of Uchiko, the fun Awa Odori Festival, and the enlightening journey of following the Shikoku pilgrimage.

The final chapter will cover Kyushu and Okinawa if you're looking for ways to enjoy a tropical paradise. These regions are some of the sunniest parts of Japan, with many ways to immerse yourself in outdoor activities and the critical historical events that shaped Japan.

Chapter 10:

The Kyushu and Okinawa Regions—Dos and Don'ts

K yushu and Okinawa are Japan's southernmost regions, offering rich history, stunning landscapes, and ancient traditions to discover. What is interesting about these two regions is that Kyushu is not only part of Japan's main islands but also includes the Ryukyu archipelago, which spans 700 miles to the southwest. Okinawa is also part of the Ryukyu archipelago, making up about two-thirds of the islands.

Discovering the Kyushu and Okinawa Regions

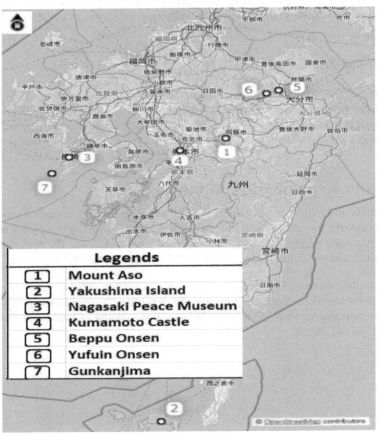

Legends	
1	Mount Aso
2	Yakushima Island
3	Nagasaki Peace Museum
4	Kumamoto Castle
5	Beppu Onsen
6	Yufuin Onsen
7	Gunkanjima

As Kyushu and Okinawa are the southernmost areas in Japan, they each have their uniqueness to discover.

While exploring Kyushu, you'll find many landscapes characterized by volcanoes, hot springs, and dense forests. These allow you to enjoy many outdoor activities, including hiking in places like Mount Aso, soaking in the hot springs in Beppu City, and exploring historic sites like Kumamoto Castle and Nagasaki's Peace Park. Okinawa, on the other hand, features stunning beaches with turquoise waters and a subtropical climate, making it ideal if you are looking to enjoy some beach relaxation. Both regions are known for their distinct culinary traditions, including the hearty ramen in Kyushu and Okinawa's unique fusion cuisine influenced by Chinese and Southeast Asian flavors.

Beyond exploring the areas of these two regions and feasting on delicious foods wherever you end up on your travels, Kyushu and Okinawa have some of the most fascinating festivals you can watch. With so much to see and do, let's plan your itinerary for this part of Japan!

What to Do in the Kyushu and Okinawa Regions

Mount Aso

Mount Aso is one of the largest active volcanoes and an iconic natural landmark in the Kyushu Region. Located in the Kumamoto Prefecture, Mount Aso is 1,592 meters tall, and its caldera, called the Aso Caldera, measures around 15 miles in diameter and is home to several peaks, craters, and active vents. The main crater, of course, is in the middle, emitting sulfurous gases and occasional volcanic ash. If you visit Mount Aso, you can explore the surrounding landscape, which will bring you through valleys and volcanic plains, allowing you to see panoramic views of the volcano. You may even see cows and horses grazing on the green grass in the surroundings of Mount Aso.

As it is an active volcano, with the most recent eruption occurring in October 2021, you may not be able to get up close to the crater.

Yakushima Island

Visiting the dense forests on Yakushima Island is like stepping into a fairytale book. This island is located off the southern coast of Kyushu and is a UNESCO World Heritage site. It is home to some of the oldest cedar trees in the world, some of which have been called *yakusugi* (a combination of the island name and "sugi," which translates to cedar) and have stood tall for over 1,000 years! There are more ancient ones in the forests that have stood longer (around 7,000 years).

Visiting this island will be a fantastic sight as you explore a network of hiking trails leading you through the moss-covered forests, past cascading waterfalls, and even to some hidden beaches, allowing you to find many opportunities for outdoor adventures and wildlife encounters. One of the parks worth exploring is Yakusugi Land, which has various hiking paths, including a boardwalk that will take you over a river. If you go to Yakasugi Land, there is a small admission fee to keep up with conservation efforts, which is ¥500 for visitors 15 years old and up. Film fans will also want to visit Shiratani Unsuikyo, the forest that inspired the 1997 film *Princess Mononoke*, directed by Hayao Miyazaki. This park is also ¥500 for visitors 15 years old and up.

Nagasaki Peace Park

Address: 9 Matsuyamamachi, Nagasaki 852-8118

On August 9, 1945, Nagasaki suffered the same fate as Hiroshima did three days earlier when an atomic bomb was dropped on the city. This park was built as a solemn memorial to commemorate the tens of thousands of lives lost and affected by the tragedy. You will find a black pillar in the park's center, marking the explosion's epicenter. Nearby is also a pillar that was a part of the former Urakami Cathedral that was destroyed when the atomic bomb detonated. If you want to see a more in-depth look at the destruction, there is also an area with a layer of soil containing the remains of broken roof tiles, bricks, and pieces of glass. Another statue worth seeing is the peace statue, which symbolizes a promise to remain peaceful.

You can also visit the Nagasaki Atomic Bomb Museum in this park. It is a sobering experience as it brings you through the devastation of the bombing as well as an opportunity to see the names of the lives lost in the memorial hall. If you plan to visit the museum, it is open from 8:30 a.m. to 6:30 p.m. (until 5:30 p.m. between September and April) and ¥200 for adults and ¥100 for teens and children.

Kumamoto Castle

Address: 1-1 Honmaru, Chuo Ward, Kumamoto 860-0002

Hours of operation: 9 a.m. to 5 p.m. daily

Kumamoto Castle is one of the grandest castles in Japan, having stood firm through the centuries. Built between 1600 and 1607 by the feudal lord Kato Kiyomasa, the castle has seen its fair share of battles and triumphs, most notably the final battle between the samurai and the ruling Meiji government in 1877. There is much history to learn when visiting this castle and seeing its distinctive black exterior and towering turrets. This is also a wonderful place to see more than 800 cherry blossom trees between March and April.

Unfortunately, the castle suffered extensive damage during the 2016 earthquakes, and restoration is underway to restore it to its former glory. If you plan to visit the castle, you can see the main keep and some grounds.

Ticket type	Price
Adults	¥800
Children (elementary and junior high school)	¥300

Beppu Onsen

Beppu Onsen is one of Japan's most famous hot spring towns, famed for its therapeutic waters and diverse bathing experiences. Some of the different bath experiences you can try are mud baths, where you soak in muddy water; sand baths, where you are buried in heated sand; and steam baths, which are heated with the hot spring's steam. Beyond the rejuvenation you can gain from this experience, Beppu also has scenic landscapes to explore.

Yufuin Onsen

Yufuin Onsen is another hot springs resort town about six miles from Beppu. It offers more opportunities to soak in the therapeutic waters and enjoy the tranquil atmosphere characterized by beautiful mountains and countryside. The town also has quaint streets lined with cafés, galleries, and boutiques selling local crafts and souvenirs.

Beyond enjoying the springs, here are a couple of other things to do in Yufuin:

- **Fairytale World at Yufuin Floral Village:** This fun theme park was inspired by Cotswold, England, and has a fantasy-like atmosphere as you explore the buildings. It is open from 9:30 a.m. to 5:30 p.m. daily and is free.
- **Visit Lake Kinrinko:** Lake Kinrinko is a beautiful lake around the town's main walking route. It is set in a crater surrounded by lovely, forested hills and Mount Yufu, a dormant volcano offering panoramic views if you hike to the summit.

Okinawa Churaumi Aquarium

Address: 424 Ishikawa, Motobu-cho, Kunigami-gun 905-0206

Hours of operation

- October to February (off-season): 8:30 a.m. to 6:30 p.m. daily (the last admission is at 5:30 p.m.)
- March to September (peak season): 8:30 a.m. to 8 p.m. daily (the last admission is at 7 p.m.)
- During August, the aquarium is open from 8:30 a.m. to 9 p.m.

Visiting an aquarium is always intriguing because it allows us to observe diverse marine life up close, including colorful fish, sharks, sea turtles, jellyfish, and more. At Okinawa Churaumi Aquarium, this renowned aquarium in the Ocean Expo Park is the largest in the world, allowing you to see a wide range of marine life—around 710 species—including tiger sharks, bull sharks, manta rays, sea turtles, and a vibrant coral reef display. At this three-floor aquarium, you'll take in all of the marine life Okinawa Churaumi Aquarium has and engage in interactive exhibits, such as touching the starfish. One of the highlights is watching the feeding times at the Kuroshio Sea Tank. Outside the aquarium are a few other marine pools where you can see dolphin shows for free.

Ticket type	Price
Adults	¥2180
High school students	¥1440
Elementary and junior high school students	¥710
Children under 6	Free

Gunkanjima

Address: 5-6 Matsugaemachi, Nagasaki 850-0921

Hours of operation: 9 a.m. to 5 p.m.

Gunkanjima, also known as Hashima Island, was once a thriving home to 5,000 people when coal was discovered in 1810. The manufacturer, Mitsubishi, bought the island and started to build its economy and small city with high-rise concrete apartment buildings resembling battleships, thus earning the nickname "Battleship Island." Unfortunately, once petroleum was discovered and the need for coal declined, the mine closed in 1974, and the inhabitants left the once thriving small metropolis behind, allowing it to fall to ruin.

The atmosphere is eerie, but it has become a popular tourist destination for exploring the abandoned island with a tour guide. These excursions are around four hours long, and you will board a boat that will take you to the island to get a glance into its former residents, the harsh living conditions, and the industrial legacy that shaped the island's landscape. In addition to admission to the island, you can explore the Gunkanjima Digital Museum, which you can do before or after the tour.

Ticket type	Price
Adults	¥1800
Students (junior high or high school students)	¥1300
Students (elementary school)	¥800
Children between 3 and 6 years old	¥500
Children under 3	Free

Shurijo Castle

Address: 1-2 Kinjo-cho, Shuri, Naha City, Okinawa 903-0815

Hours of operation

- April to June: 8 a.m. to 7:30 p.m.
- July to September: 8 a.m. to 8:30 p.m.
- October to November: 8 a.m. to 7:30 p.m.
- December to March: 8 a.m. to 6:30 p.m.

Standing atop a small hill in Naha is the iconic Shurijo Castle, a UNESCO World Heritage site symbolizing Okinawa's rich history and culture as it was the center of diplomacy and politics in the Ryukyu archipelago. Initially constructed in the 14th century, the castle was the royal residence of the Ryukyu Kingdom. It also was where many religious ceremonies took place and where artists came to hone their skills until the Ryukyu Kingdom was annexed and became a part of the Okinawa Prefecture.

The building you'll see today in Okinawa is the reconstruction of the castle rebuilt in 1992. Before then, the castle had been burned down at least times, with the last occurrence happening during World War II. Despite the damage, the castle was restored beautifully and serves as a museum where you can learn about the castle's importance to Okinawa. Additionally, you can explore the grounds and take in the sites of Naha below the hill.

Ticket type	Price
Adults	¥400
High school students	¥300
Elementary and junior high school students	¥160
Children 6 years old and under	Free

Ishigaki Island

Ishigaki Island is the largest island in the Yaeyama archipelago and Japan's tropical paradise. It boasts beautiful sandy beaches, turquoise water, and vibrant coral reefs. As such, it is a popular destination for those who love a good beach day or enjoy other outdoor activities!

Kabira Bay is one of the most popular places on Ishigaki Island, as there is plenty of opportunity for snorkeling and diving. There are also boat tours with glass bottoms that will allow you to see the reefs and ocean life below. Additionally, Kabira Bay is one of the best spots for stargazing at night without the light pollution!

Beyond Ishigaki Island's natural beauty, some historical sites are worth checking out, including the Yaeyama Museum, which has a vast display of wooden canoes, pottery, and clothing. This museum is open from 9 a.m. to 5 p.m. between Tuesday and Sunday and is ¥200 per person to enter.

What Events to Enjoy in the Kyushu and Okinawa Regions

Hakata Gion Yamakasa Festival

The Hakata Gion Yamakasa Festival is one of the most exciting events in Fukuoka's Hakata area. During this event, teams of men wearing traditional costumes race through the streets carrying a massive float called a *yamakasa*. These floats weigh around one ton, are elaborately decorated, and can be as tall as 10 meters! This festival's origins go back to around 1241, when Shoichi Kokushi, the founder of Jotenji Temple, visited Hakata to sprinkle prayer water on those affected by the plague.

The event takes place over the first two weeks of July, with various events and activities leading up to the main race. When the race happens, the teams of men carry these heavy floats on their shoulders while chanting and shouting encouragement to one another while following a course. As the teams progress, spectators throw water on the men as they pass to keep them cool.

The race is a test of strength, endurance, and teamwork. It is one of the most thrilling events to watch and not one you will want to miss if you're in Fukuoka in July!

Nagasaki Kunchi

Nagasaki Kunchi is an annual event held between October 7 and 9 in Nagasaki City from 1634. At this festival, you will find a blend of cultural influences from China and the Netherlands to celebrate Nagasaki's international port history and the cultural exchange that helped the city thrive.

If you attend this event, you can expect to witness colorful processions, dynamic dances, and elaborate performances that showcase Nagasaki's rich heritage. Some highlights include the Shishi-mai lion dance, the dragon dance, and the parade of ornate floats representing the city's different districts. In addition, there will be food vendors, and one of the snacks you should try is mochi mochi fries, which are long French fries topped with different toppings like cheese, chili, or chocolate.

Paid seating is available, but those tend to sell out fast in the weeks leading up to the event. However, the festival occurs at various venues around Nagasaki, such as the Kamome Hiroba in front of Nagasaki Station, where you won't need a ticket. You'll also be able to watch some of the floats as they parade down Nagasaki's city streets.

Naha Great Tug-of-War Festival

The Naha Great Tug-of-War Festival is an iconic event every October. This traditional festival dates back to the 17th century, when rival kingdoms competed.

Today, this event starts with a parade in the morning, complete with karate demonstrations, firecrackers, and drummers. In the afternoon, the event moves to Route 58, where 15,000 participants dressed in traditional costumes to represent the rival kingdoms face off against each other in a spectacle and then battle it out with a tug-of-war. The rope is 200 meters long and weighs around 43 tons, and each side pulls for 30 minutes or until it crosses a pre-specified distance. Everyone is welcome to join in on this event as it fosters a sense of teamwork and the spirit of overcoming obstacles together—and winning doesn't even matter!

Kumamoto Castle Festival

The Kumamoto Castle Festival is an event celebrating the history and cultural significance of the Kumamoto Castle, one of Japan's most iconic landmarks dating back to the 17th century. Despite the 2016 earthquake that rocked the Kyushu region, this festival charges onward annually in November with many activities, including traditional performances such as martial arts demonstrations and Taiko drumming, Noh theater performances, and tea ceremonies.

Where to Eat in the Kyushu and Okinawa Regions

Shikairo

Address: 4-5 Matsugaemachi, Nagasaki, 850-0921

Hours of operation: 11:30 a.m. to 3 p.m. and 5 p.m. to 8 p.m. daily

Shikairo is a longstanding restaurant in Nagasaki that has been around since 1887. This establishment specializes in serving champon, a hearty noodle dish similar to ramen served with seasonal and locally sourced ingredients in a broth made from chicken and pork bones. Prices aren't overly expensive, and it's best to eat here when the day is clear and sunny, as you will get to enjoy stunning views of the surrounding areas as you enjoy your meal.

Grill Mitsuba

Address: 1-4-31 Kitahama, Beppu, Oita Prefecture 874-0920

Hours of operation: 11:30 to 2 p.m. and 6 p.m. to 9 p.m. (closed Tuesdays and on Mondays for dinner)

If you're exploring Beppu for its bathhouses, you should visit Grill Misuba to enjoy a bite. This restaurant has been around for over 60 years and is well-loved for its signature Bungo beef steak. The restaurant is cozy, with every patron sitting at a countertop watching the chef work his culinary magic to create different dishes.

Blue Seal Ice Cream Parlor

Address: 1-2-32 Makishi, Naha City, Okinawa Prefecture

Hours of operation: 11 a.m. to 9 p.m. daily

Are you in the mood for a sweet treat? Blue Seal Ice Cream Parlor has roots in America, but this ice cream parlor has upped the soft-serve ice cream game by offering innovative flavors alongside the classics. The menu features more than 30 flavors made with local ingredients, which you can enjoy on a cone or in a cup.

Makishi Public Market

Address: 2 Chome-10-1 Matsuo, Naha, Okinawa 900-0014

Hours of operation: 8 a.m. to 9 p.m. daily

Makishi Public Market is a bustling market in Naha and a place for Okinawa locals to get a peek into everyday life. This market sells everything from fresh produce to meat, fish, and other general merchandise. However, there are also food vendors throughout the market offering a wide range of food options, including tempura and steamed cakes.

Hakata Chikusai

Address: 4-8 Tenyamachi 1F Chowa Bldg., Hakata, Fukuoka, Fukuoka Prefecture 812-0025

Hours of operation: 11:30 a.m. to 3 p.m. and 6 p.m. to 10 p.m.

At Hakata Chikusai, you can feast on delicious Japanese and teppanyaki dishes in a relaxed atmosphere. You can watch the chefs make your meal at a counter seat at this establishment. Eating here is a bit pricier (around ¥8000 if you go for dinner), but the lovely atmosphere is worth it!

What to Eat in the Kyushu and Okinawa Regions

Tonkotsu Ramen

Kyushu is famous for its tonkotsu ramen, a rich and flavorful noodle soup made with a creamy broth derived from pork bones. The noodles are typically served with toppings like sliced pork belly, green onions, and pickled ginger. Fukuoka City, in particular, is renowned for its Hakata-style tonkotsu ramen, characterized by its thin, straight noodles and intensely porky broth.

Karashi Mentaiko

Karashi mentaiko is a spicy marinated cod roe that originated in Fukuoka Prefecture. The roe is marinated in a mixture of chili peppers, salt, and sometimes other seasonings, giving it a fiery and umami-rich flavor. Karashi mentaiko is often served as a topping for rice, pasta, or sandwiches, and it's a popular ingredient in Kyushu cuisine.

Motsunabe

 Motsunabe is a hearty hotpot dish made with beef or pork offal (motsu) simmered in a savory broth with vegetables, tofu, and other ingredients. It's a popular dish in Fukuoka Prefecture, particularly during the colder months. Motsunabe is enjoyed as a communal meal shared among friends and family, often accompanied by cold beer or shochu (Japanese distilled spirit).

Okinawan Soba

Okinawan soba is a distinct style of noodle soup made with wheat noodles in a clear, bonito-based broth. Unlike traditional Japanese soba noodles, Okinawan soba noodles are thicker and have a chewier texture. The soup is typically topped with slices of tender pork belly, green onions, and red pickled ginger. Okinawan soba is a beloved comfort food in Okinawa Prefecture, enjoyed by locals and visitors alike.

Goya Champuru

Goya champuru is a classic Okinawan stir-fry dish made with bitter melon (goya), tofu, eggs, and pork or ham. The bitter melon is sliced thinly and stir-fried with other ingredients in a savory sauce, resulting in a flavorful and nutritious dish. Goya champuru is a staple of Okinawan home cooking and is often served as a side dish or main course.

Where to Stay in the Kyushu and Okinawa Regions

Yufuin Onsen Tsukanoma

Address: 444-3 Yufuincho Kawakami, Yufu, Oita 879-5102

Yufuin Onsen Tsukanoma is a lovely Japanese inn in the picturesque town of Yufuin. This beautiful accommodation is nestled on the edge of the scenic Mount Yofu, offering stunning views of the lush greenery outside that creates a serene and rejuvenating atmosphere. In this ryokan, you can expect guest rooms with tatami floors, sliding doors, and futon beds to provide an authentic Japanese experience. As a guest, you're welcome to unwind in their hot spring bath and the public bath to absorb the therapeutic properties of the waters. Additionally, an excellent on-site restaurant offers multicourse *kaiseki* dinners and breakfasts. This is a lovely getaway in the Kyushu experience, where you can relax.

Hilton Fukuoka Sea Hawk

Address: 2 Chome-2-3 Jigyōhama, Chuo Ward, Fukuoka 810-8650

Hilton Fukuoka Sea Hawk is an upscale hotel overlooking the picturesque Hakata Bay, offering a range of accommodation options, from simple guest rooms to spacious suites. With the hotel being on the waterfront, you can take in beautiful views of the bay and city skyline from your room or if you dine in one of the hotel's restaurants. This is a great place to stay if you intend to go to the Hakata Gion Yamakasa Festival and visit other attractions the city offers, such as Fukuoka Castle.

Hotel Wing Port Nagasaki

Address: 9-2 Daikokumachi, Nagasaki 850-0057

Hotel Wing Port Nagasaki is a comfortable and budget-friendly accommodation offering compact rooms for travelers seeking basic rooms. This hotel comes with a kettle, free coffee, and a fridge in the rooms. It's also a short distance to several of Nagasaki's attractions, including Nagasaki Peace Park.

Kanehide Kise Beach Palace

Address: 115-2 Kise, Nago, Okinawa 905-0026

Kanehide Kise Beach Palace is a stunning beachfront resort located in the northern part of Okinawa. This luxury resort offers a tranquil retreat where you can fully relax in your elegant guest rooms or enjoy time on the private beach. The resort offers a wide range of activities for its guests to enjoy, including snorkeling or wakeboarding.

Hostel Casa Noda

Address: 6-1-3F Motofune-cho, Nagasaki City, Nagasaki Prefecture 850-0035

Hostel Casa Noda is a cozy and welcoming hostel located in the heart of Nagasaki City. It is within walking distance of several attractions, including Nagasaki Peace

Park, making it an excellent base for exploring the city. If you stay here, you can choose between a dormitory-style room or a private room. The facility also has a washing machine if you need to do laundry.

What Not to Do in the Kyushu and Okinawa Regions

Don't Ignore No-Entry Zones at Mount Aso

As Mount Aso is an active volcano, no-entry zones may be posted occasionally based on volcanic activity, which means you won't be able to see the crater. While volcanoes are fascinating—especially when there is an increase in volcanic activity—don't ignore the no-entry zones posted. They are there for everyone's safety! Be sure to check Mount Aso volcano's state before going. (However, even if you can't get close to the crater, it is still worth visiting and admiring the volcanic peaks.)

Take Note of Repair activities at Kumamoto Castle.

Kumamoto Castle may have areas that are under repair or restoration, as it was damaged by earthquakes in recent years. Pay attention to any safety warnings, barriers, or signage indicating restricted areas, and avoid entering off-limits zones for your safety and the preservation of the site.

Don't Ignore Safety Warnings at Gunkanjima

Gunkanjima is an abandoned island with deteriorating buildings and structures. Respect any safety warnings, barriers, or restricted areas indicated by signs or guides. Avoid entering off-limits zones, as they may pose hazards such as collapsing buildings or unstable terrain. Gunkanjima is home to various artifacts and remnants of its industrial past. Avoid removing or tampering with any artifacts, relics, or historical materials on the island. Leave them undisturbed to maintain the integrity of the site and its historical context. Certain items, such as drones, alcohol, or large bags, may not be allowed on the island.

Your Japanese Adventure Awaits!

Okinawa and Kyushu boast of new adventures and landscapes thanks to being in the southernmost part of Japan. Visiting these regions will not only allow you to soak up the Japanese lifestyle between their many hot springs, but it's also a place where you can immerse yourself in their rich heritage through their interesting festivals. These two areas aren't areas many might think of visiting, but now that you know what you can do in this part of Japan, I hope it will make it on your trip itinerary, if not your trip bucket list.

Conclusion

J apan is one of the most beautiful and exciting countries to visit, especially since its culture differs from ours. Throughout this book, we have explored many parts of Japan worth visiting so that you can immerse yourself in their culture and have an authentic experience rather than one filled with tourist traps. There will be hundreds of tourist attractions you should visit. Still, we have covered many that can take you beyond those "essential" attractions, allowing you to finalize your itinerary from start to finish with the necessary information you need.

Now that you have the knowledge and insider tips, it's time to prepare for your Japanese adventure with complete confidence and excitement. Whether you'll immerse yourself in the hustle and bustle of Japanese cities like Tokyo, soak in the therapeutic waters at a hot spring, or immerse yourself in rich cultural experiences, Japan is there waiting for you to touch down to start your journey. Also, remember to take the lessons you have learned in this travel guide as you wander through the ancient sites and areas with historical significance. This is the time to make unforgettable memories, so embrace every moment and let Japan leave a mark on your heart.

If this book has helped you begin to plan your Japanese adventure, please help other fellow travelers by leaving a review on Amazon.

Glossary

It never hurts to learn a few phrases ahead of your trip! Here are some great starters to help you communicate while in Japan.

- **Can I check my bag?:** Watashi no baggu o shirabete mo īdesu ka?

- **Can I get a matcha tea?:** Matcha o moraemasu ka?

- **Can I get room service?:** Rūmusābisu wa riyō dekimasu ka?

- **Goodbye:** Sayōnara

- **Hello:** Konnichiwa

- **I would like to check in:** Chekkuin shitai nodesuga.

- **I would like to check out** Chekkuauto shitai nodesuga.

- **Onsen:** Hot spring

- **Please:** Onegaishimasu

- **Thank you:** Arigatō

- **Where is the bus station?:** Basutei wa tokodesu ka?

References

A guide to Asakusa – an area of true Japanese tradition. (2022, October 19). Go Tokyo. https://www.gotokyo.org/en/destinations/eastern-tokyo/asakusa/index.html

A guide to the best airline to fly to Japan. (n.d.). Next Vacay. https://nextvacay.com/best-airline-to-fly-to-japan

About Shurijo Castle. (n.d.). Shurijo Castle Park. https://oki-park.jp/shurijo/en/about

Accommodation in Japan. (n.d.). Japan Experience. https://www.japan-experience.com/plan-your-trip/thematic-guides/accommodation-in-japan

Adventure out to Gunkanjima (Battleship Island). (n.d.). Japan Cheapo. https://japancheapo.com/tours/adventure-gunkanjima-aka-battleship-island

Akashi Kaikyo Bridge. (n.d.). Japan-Guide.com. https://www.japan-guide.com/e/e3559.html

Alyse. (2024, February 2). *Honest advice for first-time travelers and repeat travelers on where to stay in Tokyo.* The Invisible Tourist. https://www.theinvisibletourist.com/where-to-stay-in-tokyo

Aoba Castle. (n.d.). Japan-Guide.com. https://www.japan-guide.com/e/e5152.html

Aokigahara Forest. (n.d.). Japan National Tourism Organization (Official Site). https://www.japan.travel/en/spot/1335

Aomoriya. (n.d.). Hoshino Resorts Aomoriya. https://hoshinoresorts.com/en/hotels/aomoriya

APA Hotel Kyoto Gion Excellent. (n.d.). Booking.com. https://www.booking.com/hotel/jp/kyoto-gion.en-gb.html

Asahikawa Winter Festival. (n.d.-a). Japan National Tourism Organization. https://www.japan.travel/en/spot/470

Asahikawa Winter Festival. (n.d.-b). Japan-Guide.com. https://www.japan-guide.com/e/e6894.html

Asahikawa Winter Festival. (n.d.-c). JapanTravel. https://en.japantravel.com/hokkaido/asahikawa-winter-festival/33920

Asakusa. (n.d.). Japan-Guide.com. https://www.japan-guide.com/e/e3004.html

Asakusa Kokono Club Hotel. (n.d.). Booking.com. https://www.booking.com/hotel/jp/qian-cao-jiu-ju-le-bu-dong-jing-du-tai-dong-qu.en-gb.html

asiatravelbug. (2023, December 28). *Where to stay in Tokyo [7 best areas for tourists to stay in Tokyo].* https://asiatravelbug.com/blog/where-to-stay-in-tokyo-first-time-best-area-family

Awa Odori. (n.d.). Japan-Guide.com. https://www.japan-guide.com/e/e7802.html

Awa Odori Festival. (n.d.). Japan National Tourism Organization. https://www.japan.travel/en/spot/203

Banquet. (n.d.). Yamagyu. https://www.yamagyu.com/menu/enkai.html

Bartok, M. (2014, November 7). *Shikairo.* JapanTravel. https://en.japantravel.com/nagasaki/shikairo/16290

Baseel, C. (2019, August 29). *15 rude things not to do on trains in Japan [survey].* SoraNews24. https://soranews24.com/2019/08/29/15-rude-things-not-to-do-on-trains-in-japan%E3%80%90survey%E3%80%91

Becki and Shawn. (n.d.). *Exchanging money in Japan.* Japan and More. https://japanandmore.com/travel-tips/money-in-japan

Best time to visit Japan: When to go & when to avoid! (2024, February 1). Two Wandering Soles. https://www.twowanderingsoles.com/blog/best-time-to-visit-japan

Bike Tour Japan. (n.d.). *Cycling in Japan.* Epic Road Rides. https://epicroadrides.com/destinations/cycling-japan

Bureau, T. C. & V. (n.d.). *Winter illumination guide.* Go Tokyo. https://www.gotokyo.org/en/story/guide/winter-illuminationn-guide/index.html

Buy your JR pass. (n.d.). Japan RailPass. https://www.jrailpass.com/the-japan-rail-pass

Carrying on the flavors developed by his grandfather. (n.d.). Beppu. https://beppu.asia/en/spot/6022

Cawood, C. (2016, November 23). *Naruto whirlpools from the bridge.* JapanTravel. https://en.japantravel.com/tokushima/naruto-whirlpools-from-the-bridge/33226

Chanson, H. (2023, September 24). *Whirlpools: Experiencing Naruto whirlpools.* https://staff.civil.uq.edu.au/h.chanson/whirlpl.html

Cheapo, J. (n.d.). *Sapporo Summer Festival.* Japan Cheapo. https://japancheapo.com/events/sapporo-summer-festival

Chubu. (n.d.). Japanko Official. https://japanko-official.com/chubu

Chubu region. (n.d.). Unfamiliar Japan Tours. https://uj-tours.com/chubu-region

Chugoku Region. (n.d.). JapanTravel. https://en.japantravel.com/regions/chugoku

Churaumi Aquarium. (n.d.). Japan-Guide.com. https://www.japan-guide.com/e/e7109.html

Comfort Hotel Hiroshima Otemachi. (n.d.). Booking.com. https://www.booking.com/hotel/jp/comfort-hiroshima-otemachi.en-gb.html

Comfort Hotel Toyama. (n.d.). Booking.com. https://www.booking.com/hotel/jp/comfort-toyama.en-gb.html

Complete guide to the Meiji Jingu Shrine. (2023, June 27). Japan Wonder Travel Blog. https://blog.japanwondertravel.com/visit-meiji-jingu-shrine-23658

Coppola, R. (n.d.). *Roman Coppola quotes.* BrainyQuote. https://www.brainyquote.com/quotes/roman_coppola_492105

Cosmos Guesthouse. (n.d.). Booking.com. https://www.booking.com/hotel/jp/gesutohausu-kosumosu.en-gb.html

Crossley-Baxter, L. (n.d.). *The Philosopher's Path: A spiritual, seasonal stroll.* Japan Cheapo. https://japancheapo.com/entertainment/philosophers-path-kyoto

Custom & manners. (n.d.). Japan National Tourism Organization. https://www.japan.travel/en/plan/custom-manners

Daiwa Roynet Hotel Chiba Ekimae. (n.d.). Booking.com. https://www.booking.com/hotel/jp/daiwa-roynet-chiba-ekimae.en-gb.html

Dayman, L. (n.d.). *Gion Kyoto: 20 must-see highlights of the geisha district*. Japan Objects. https://japanobjects.com/features/gion-kyoto

Dayman, L. (2021, June 28). *Mount Koya: A visitor's guide to Japan's most sacred site*. Japan Cheapo. https://japancheapo.com/entertainment/mount-koya-day-trip

Domestic air travel. (n.d.). Japan-Guide.com. https://www.japan-guide.com/e/e2365.html

Dorsey, A. (2024, March 2). *47 facts about Hiroshima*. Facts.net. https://facts.net/world/cities/47-facts-about-hiroshima

Ebisawa, A. (n.d.). Oda Nobunaga. In *Encyclopædia Britannica*. Retrieved March 12, 2024, from https://www.britannica.com/biography/Oda-Nobunaga

Eighteen restaurants are located in Tokyo that offer terrific food. (2020, January 16). Will Fly for Food. https://www.willflyforfood.net/tokyo-food-guide-18-must-eat-restaurants-in-tokyo-japan

Enright, B. (n.d.). *What is Tokyo like? Things to love about Japan's capital city*. Borders of Adventure. https://www.bordersofadventure.com/what-is-tokyo-like

Erin. (2019, December 16). *Where to stay in Japan: The ultimate guide to Japan accommodation*. Never Ending Voyage. https://www.neverendingvoyage.com/where-to-stay-in-japan-accommodation-options

Erin. (2023, March 2). *26 cool things to do in Tokyo, Japan (2024)*. Never Ending Voyage. https://www.neverendingvoyage.com/cool-things-to-do-in-tokyo

Experience fruit picking in Tohoku region. (n.d.). Japan Fruits. https://japan-harvest.jp/fruits/en/feature/tohoku

Expert tips for your Japan packing list. (n.d.). Boutique Japan. https://boutiquejapan.com/japan-travel-tips-packing-for-japan

Explore Ise-Shima National Park. (n.d.). National Parks of Japan. https://www.japan.travel/national-parks/parks/ise-shima/explore

Explore Makishi Public Market. (n.d.). Okinawa Island Guide. https://www.oki-islandguide.com/areaguide/explore-makishi-public-market

Explore the Fuji Five Lakes. (n.d.). Japan National Tourism Organization. Retrieved March 14, 2024, from https://www.japan.travel/en/itineraries/fuji-five-lakes-itinerary

Exploring the soul of Japanese sake breweries across the Tohoku Region. (2022, January). Japan National Tourism Organization. https://www.japan.travel/en/japan-magazine/2201_exploring-soul-japanese-sake-breweries-across-tohoku-region

ezhuterp93. (2019, September 10). *Review of one-michelin star restaurant, Sushi Arai*. Food and Miles. https://foodandmiles.blog/2019/09/10/review-of-one-michelin-star-restaurant-sushi-arai

Fares and hours. (n.d.). Miyajima Ropeway. https://miyajima-ropeway.info/english/fares-and-hours

Fitzsimons, J. (2023, September 1). *Tips for visiting Mount Fuji in spring*. Indiana Jo. https://indianajo.com/how-not-to-visit-mount-fuji-in-spring/#Dont_assume_seeing_Mount_Fuji_is_more_likely_at_Mount_Fuji_than_Tokyo

Follow Me Away. (2019, April 5). *7 big mistakes to avoid when planning A trip to Japan*. https://www.followmeaway.com/planning-a-trip-to-japan

Four Seasons Hotel Kyoto. (n.d.). Booking.com. https://www.booking.com/hotel/jp/four-seasons-kyoto.en-gb.html

Furano flower fields. (n.d.). Japan-Guide.com. https://www.japan-guide.com/e/e6826.html

Fushimi Inari Shrine. (n.d.). Japan-Guide.com. https://www.japan-guide.com/e/e3915.html

Fushimi Inari Taisha Shrine. (n.d.). Japan National Tourism Organization (Official Site). https://www.japan.travel/en/spot/1128

Gakuran, M. (2010, June 28). *Gunkanjima: Ruins of a forbidden island*. Gakuranman. https://gakuran.com/gunkanjima-ruins-of-a-forbidden-island

Garden. (n.d.). Meiji Jingu. https://www.meijijingu.or.jp/en/whattosee/garden

General information. (n.d.). Matsumoto Castle. https://www.matsumoto-castle.jp/eng/info

Get a taste of Okinawa with Blue Seal Ice Cream. (n.d.). Japan National Tourism Organization. https://www.japan.travel/en/my/travelers-blog/born-america-raised-okinawa-ice-cream

Getting here, admission & hours. (n.d.). Tokyo National Museum. https://www.tnm.jp/modules/r_free_page/index.php?id=113

Gifu Nobunaga Festival. (n.d.). Visit Gifu. https://visitgifu.com/see-do/gifu-nobunaga-festival

Gillett, K. (2023, December 13). *Why does everyone want to travel to Japan in 2024?* The National. https://www.thenationalnews.com/travel/2023/12/13/travel-trends-japan-destinations-2024

Ginkakuji (Silver Pavilion). (n.d.). Japan-Guide.com. https://www.japan-guide.com/e/e3907.html

Ginza. (n.d.). Japan-Guide.com. https://www.japan-guide.com/e/e3005.html

Guesthouse AntHut. (n.d.). Booking.com. https://www.booking.com/hotel/jp/guesthouse-anthut.en-gb.html

Guide to living in Japan: Train and bus etiquette. (n.d.). Japan Study Abroad Network. https://jpn-study.com/guide-to-living-in-japan-train-bus-etiquette

Gunkanjima: Hashima Island. (n.d.). Haikyo: Abandoned Japan. https://haikyo.org/gunkanjima-hashima-island

Gyutan. (n.d.). Japan-Guide.com. https://www.japan-guide.com/e/e5157.html

Hachimantai. (n.d.). Japan-Guide.com. https://www.japan-guide.com/e/e3651.html

Hakata Gion Yamakasa Festival. (n.d.-a). Japan National Tourism Organization. https://www.japan.travel/en/spot/269

Hakata Gion Yamakasa Festival. (n.d.-b). SnapJapan. https://www.snapjapan.com/event/hakata-gion-yamakasa-festival

Hakata Gion Yamakasa, UNESCO Intangible Cultural Heritage, is about to start this year again! (n.d.). Fukuoka City Guide. https://yokanavi.com/en/event/124458

Hanatoro. (n.d.). Traditional Kyoto. https://traditionalkyoto.com/activities/hanatoro

Hanus, J. (2022, August 30). *Autumn festivals in Kumamoto Prefecture*. H&R Group. https://morethanrelo.com/en/autumn-festivals-in-kumamoto-prefecture

Health and safety on the Shikoku Pilgrimage. (n.d.). Henro. https://www.henro.org/shikoku-pilgrimage/health-safety

Hida Furukawa. (n.d.). Japan National Tourism Organization. https://www.japan.travel/en/spot/2032

Hida-Furukawa. (n.d.). Japan-Guide.com. https://www.japan-guide.com/e/e5975.html

Highway buses. (n.d.). Japan-Guide.com. https://www.japan-guide.com/e/e2366.html

Hilton Fukuoka Sea Hawk. (n.d.). Booking.com. https://www.booking.com/hotel/jp/hilton-fukuoka-sea-hawk.en-gb.html

Hiraizumi (UNESCO). (n.d.). Japan National Tourism Organization. https://www.japan.travel/en/world-heritage/hiraizumi

Hirosaki Castle. (n.d.). Japan-Guide.com. https://www.japan-guide.com/e/e3700.html

Hiroshima Carps baseball - an experience you will not soon forget. (n.d.). Travel Dudes. https://traveldudes.com/hiroshima-carps-baseball-an-experience-you-will-not-soon-forget

Hiroshima Castle. (n.d.). Japan-Guide.com. https://www.japan-guide.com/e/e3402.html

Hiroshima City Museum of Contemporary Art (Hiroshima MOCA) - Directory - e-flux. (n.d.). E-Flux Directory. https://www.e-flux.com/directory/73328/hiroshima-city-museum-of-contemporary-art-hiroshima-moca

Hiroshima Flower Festival. (n.d.-a). Chugoku Region Tourism Guide. https://www.into-you.jp/en/places/3471

Hiroshima Flower Festival. (n.d.-b). JapanTravel. https://en.japantravel.com/hiroshima/hiroshima-flower-festival/1345

Hiroshima Peace Memorial Ceremony. (n.d.). Japan National Tourism Organization. https://www.japan.travel/en/spot/161

Hiroshima Washington Hotel. (n.d.). Booking.com. https://www.booking.com/hotel/jp/hiroshima-washington.en-gb.html

History of Senso-ji. (n.d.). Asakusa Kannon Senso-Ji. https://www.senso-ji.jp/english

Hostel Casa Noda. (n.d.). Booking.com. https://www.booking.com/hotel/jp/hostel-casa-noda.en-gb.html

Hot spring. (n.d.). Akiu Onsen. https://www.akiu-rantei.com/en/onsen/#sec01

Hot spring baths (onsen). (n.d.). Japan-Guide.com. https://www.japan-guide.com/e/e4701.html

Hotel Crown Hills Yamagata. (n.d.). Booking.com. https://www.booking.com/hotel/jp/crown-hills-yamagata.en-gb.html

Hotel Granvia Hiroshima. (n.d.). Booking.com. https://www.booking.com/hotel/jp/granvia-hiroshima.en-gb.html

Hotel Metropolitan Nagano. (n.d.). Booking.com. https://www.booking.com/hotel/jp/metropolitan-nagano-nagano.en-gb.html

Hotel Metropolitan Tokyo Ikebukuro. (n.d.). Tripadvisor. https://www.tripadvisor.ca/Hotel_Review-g1066460-d304546-Reviews-Hotel_Metropolitan_Tokyo_Ikebukuro-Toshima_Tokyo_Prefecture_Kanto.html

Hotel Neu Schloss Otaru. (n.d.). Booking.com. https://www.booking.com/hotel/jp/hotel-neuschloss.en-gb.html

Hotel Nikko Niigata. (n.d.). Booking.com. https://www.booking.com/hotel/jp/nikko-niigata.en-gb.html

Hotel Nord Otaru. (n.d.). Booking.com. https://www.booking.com/hotel/jp/nord-otaru.en-gb.html

Hotel Towadaso. (n.d.). Booking.com. https://www.booking.com/hotel/jp/towadaso.en-gb.html

Hotel Wing Port Nagasaki. (n.d.). Booking.com. https://www.booking.com/hotel/jp/wing-port-nagasaki.en-gb.html

Hours and admission. (n.d.-a). Hiroshima Peace Memorial Museum. https://hpmmuseum.jp/modules/info/index.php?action=PageView&page_id=47&lang=eng

Hours and admission. (n.d.-b). Itsukushima Shrine. https://www.itsukushimajinja.jp/en/admission.html

Hours of operation. (n.d.). Okinawa Churaumi Aquarium. https://churaumi.okinawa/en/guide/hour

How to find cheap flights to Japan? Japan travel blog. (n.d.). Flashpacking Japan. https://www.flashpackingjapan.com/japan-travel/how-to-find-cheap-flights-to-japan

Imada, K. (2023, March 9). *How to rent a car in Japan: where to go and what you'll need*. TimeOut. https://www.timeout.com/tokyo/travel/how-to-rent-a-car-in-japan-where-to-go-and-what-youll-need

Important to know about Dotonbori. (2023, February 14). Lestacworld.com. https://lestacworld.com/asia/japan/osaka/important-to-know-about-dotonbori/?currency=CAD

Inaka-ya. (n.d.). Fodor's Travel. https://www.fodors.com/world/asia/japan/the-japan-alps-and-the-north-chubu-coast/restaurants/reviews/inaka-ya-448111

Information user's guide. (n.d.). Gunkanjima Digital Museum. https://www.gunkanjima-museum.jp/data/information/

Interesting facts about Kyoto. (n.d.). Big 7 Enjoy Travel. https://www.enjoytravel.com/au/travel-news/interehis%20osting-facts/interesting-facts-kyoto

International air travel. (n.d.). Japan-Guide.com. https://www.japan-guide.com/e/e2034.html

Introduction of Kyoto. (n.d.). Sharing Kyoto. https://sharing-kyoto.com/guide/introduction

Is it safe to travel to Japan? (n.d.). Intrepid Travel. https://www.intrepidtravel.com/nl/japan/is-it-safe-to-travel-to-japan

Ishigaki Island. (n.d.-a). Japan-Guide.com. https://www.japan-guide.com/e/e7201.html

Ishigaki Island. (n.d.-b). Visit Okinawa Japan. https://visitokinawajapan.com/destinations/yaeyama-islands/ishigaki-island

Itsukushima Shrine. (n.d.). Japan-Guide.com. https://www.japan-guide.com/e/e3450.html

Iya Valley. (n.d.). Japan-Guide.com. https://www.japan-guide.com/e/e7827.html

JAL Editorial Staff. (n.d.-a). *The ultimate travel guide to visiting Tokyo Station*. Japan Airlines. https://www.jal.co.jp/at/en/guide-to-japan/destinations/articles/tokyo/tokyo-station.html

JAL Editorial Staff. (n.d.-b). *Understanding the climate, seasons, and weather in Japan*. Japan Airlines. https://www.jal.co.jp/nl/en/guide-to-japan/plan-your-trip/tips/the-climate-seasons-and-weather-in-japan.html

Japan. (n.d.-a). National Geographic Kids. https://kids.nationalgeographic.com/geography/countries/article/japan

Japan. (n.d.-b). Power Plugs & Sockets of the World. https://www.power-plugs-sockets.com/ca/japan

Japan Experience. (2012a, December 27). *Ferries in Japan*. https://www.japan-experience.com/plan-your-trip/to-know/traveling-japan/japan-ferry

Japan Experience. (2012b, December 27). *Fushimi Inari Shrine*. https://www.japan-experience.com/all-about-japan/kyoto/temples-shrines/fushimi-inari-kyoto

Japan international travel information. (n.d.). Travel.State.Gov. https://travel.state.gov/content/travel/en/international-travel/International-Travel-Country-Information-Pages/Japan.html

Japan local railways. (n.d.). Japan National Tourism Organization (Official Site). https://www.japan.travel/en/plan/getting-around/other-local-railways

Japan Travel Staff. (2019, August 7). *How to rent a bike in Japan*. JapanTravel. https://en.japantravel.com/guide/how-to-rent-a-bike-in-japan/59041

Japan's Mt Aso erupts, people warned to stay away. (2021, October 20). Aljazeera. https://www.aljazeera.com/news/2021/10/20/refile-japans-mount-aso-erupts-people-warned-to-stay-away

Japanese fireworks: The best 8 hanabi festivals to visit. (2023, January 5). Japan Rail Pass. https://www.jrailpass.com/blog/japanese-fireworks-hanabi-festivals

Japanese personalities & culture: Getting along in Japan. (2023, May 29). Japan Living Guide. https://www.japanlivingguide.com/living-in-japan/culture/japanese-personalities-culture-getting-along

Japanese travel words and vocabulary. (n.d.). Learn Japanese Adventure. https://www.learn-japanese-adventure.com/japanese-travel-words.html

Japan's Regions: Kyushu & Okinawa. (n.d.). Japan Experience. https://www.japan-experience.com/plan-your-trip/to-know/traveling-japan/kyushu-okinawa

Jean. (2016, July 1). *Japan – Hiroshima Food Festival*. Wansato. https://www.wansato.com/japan-hiroshima-food-festival

Jidai Matsuri character guide. (n.d.). Discover Kyoto. https://www.discoverkyoto.com/kyoto-voice/jidai-matsuri-history

Jigokudani (Hell Valley). (n.d.). Japan-Guide.com. https://www.japan-guide.com/e/e6751.html

Joy, A. (2017, November 22). *11 places you should avoid on any trip to Tokyo*. Culture Trip. https://theculturetrip.com/asia/japan/articles/11-places-you-should-avoid-on-any-trip-to-tokyo

Kanazawa. (n.d.). Japan-Guide.com. https://www.japan-guide.com/e/e2167.html

Kanehide Kise Beach Palace. (n.d.). Booking.com. https://www.booking.com/hotel/jp/kise-beach-palace.en-gb.html

Kansai region: Japan travel guide. (n.d.). Japan Rail Pass. https://www.jrailpass.com/blog/regions-of-japan/kansai

Kanto region. (n.d.). Japan-Guide.com. https://www.japan-guide.com/list/e1103.html

Kazurabashi Bridge. (n.d.). Japan-Guide.com. https://www.japan-guide.com/e/e7828.html

Keio Plaza Hotel Sapporo. (n.d.). Booking.com. https://www.booking.com/hotel/jp/keio-plaza-sapporo.en-gb.html

Kenrokuen Garden. (n.d.). Japan-Guide.com. https://www.japan-guide.com/e/e4200.html

Kenzia V. (2022, April 28). *Popular events and festivals in Tokyo to experience*. GoWithGuide. https://gowithguide.com/blog/popular-events-and-festivals-in-tokyo-to-experience-3057

Kinkakuji (Golden Pavilion). (n.d.). Japan-Guide.com. https://www.japan-guide.com/e/e3908.html

Kirkland, C. (2023, January 22). *Tokyo accommodation guide: Budget hotels and other options*. Tokyo Cheapo. https://tokyocheapo.com/accommodationcat/accommodation-guide

Kiso Valley. (n.d.). Japan-Guide.com. https://www.japan-guide.com/e/e6075.html

Kitano-cho. (n.d.). Japan-Guide.com. https://www.japan-guide.com/e/e3550.html

Kiyomizu-dera Temple. (n.d.). Kyoto City Official Travel Guide. https://kyoto.travel/en/shrine_temple/131.html

Klook Team. (2024, January 22). *Welcome Suica IC Card complete guide: Easy travel with this prepaid card*. Klook. https://www.klook.com/en-CA/blog/welcome-suica-card-guide

Kobe. (n.d.). Japan-Guide.com. https://www.japan-guide.com/e/e2159.html

Kobe Meriken Park Oriental Hotel. (n.d.). Booking.com. https://www.booking.com/hotel/jp/kobe-meriken-park-oriental.en-gb.html

Kokeshi dolls - an in-depth guide. (n.d.). Mingei Arts. https://mingeiarts.com/pages/kokeshi-dolls

Kompirasan. (n.d.). Japan-Guide.com. https://www.japan-guide.com/e/e5451.html

Konpira Shrine. (n.d.). Shikoku Tours. https://shikokutours.com/points-of-interest/kagawa/konpira-shrine

Korakuen Garden. (n.d.). Japan-Guide.com. https://www.japan-guide.com/e/e5701.html

Kumamoto Castle. (n.d.-a). Webket. https://webket.jp/pc/ticket/index?fc=80006&ac=7001

Kumamoto Castle. (n.d.-b). Japan-Guide.com. https://www.japan-guide.com/e/e4501.html

Kura-Zushi. (n.d.). Tripadvisor. https://www.tripadvisor.fr/Restaurant_Review-g298239-d13939674-Reviews-Kura_Zushi-Akita_Akita_Prefecture_Tohoku.html

Kyoto Imperial Palace. (n.d.). The Imperial Household Agency. https://sankan.kunaicho.go.jp/multilingual/lang/en/information.html

Kyoto Imperial Palace and Kyoto Gyoen National Garden. (n.d.). Discover Kyoto. https://www.discoverkyoto.com/places-go/gosho

Lake Tazawa. (n.d.-a). GaijinPot Travel. https://travel.gaijinpot.com/lake-tazawa

Lake Tazawa. (n.d.-b). Japan-Guide.com. https://www.japan-guide.com/e/e3657.html

Lake Tazawa's scenery. (n.d.). Semboku City. https://www.city.semboku.akita.jp/en/sightseeing/spot/04_tazawako.html

Lake Toya (Toyako). (n.d.). Japan-Guide.com. https://www.japan-guide.com/e/e6725.html

Lukiih. (2024, January 13). *Etiquette in Japan: 13 things tourists should not do*. Lists by Lukiih. https://listsbylukiih.com/japan-cultural-differences

MacEacheran, M. (2018, January 4). *The Japanese castle that defied history*. BBC. https://www.bbc.com/travel/article/20180103-the-japanese-castle-that-defied-history

Masafumi A. (2023, March 8). *10 reasons why Japan should be your next travel destination*. LinkedIn. https://www.linkedin.com/pulse/10-reasons-why-japan-should-your-next-travel-destination-arai

Matcha Admin. (2024, January 19). *Hokkaido's best 30 restaurants in Japan 2024*. Matcha. https://matcha-jp.com/en/10680

Matcha_En. (2023, December 20). *20 exciting things to do in Asakusa - 2024 guide*. MATCHA. https://matcha-jp.com/en/5112

Matsumoto Castle. (n.d.). Japan-Guide.com. https://www.japan-guide.com/e/e6051.html

Matsumoto Hotel Kagetsu. (n.d.). Booking.com. https://www.booking.com/hotel/jp/matsumoto-kagetsu.en-gb.html

Matsushima Bay. (n.d.). Japan-Guide.com. https://www.japan-guide.com/e/e5101.html

Matsuyama Castle. (n.d.-a). The Official Website of Tourism Matsuyama. https://en.matsuyama-sightseeing.com/spot/1-2

Matsuyama Castle. (n.d.-b). Japan-Guide.com. https://www.japan-guide.com/e/e5501.html

Meiji Jingu Museum. (n.d.). Meiji Jingu. https://www.meijijingu.or.jp/en/whattosee/museum

Meiji Shrine. (n.d.). Japan-Guide.com. https://www.japan-guide.com/e/e3002.html

Melissa. (2024, February 13). *Tokyo Disneyland guide: How to optimize your visit and minimize wait time!* Girl Eat World. https://girleatworld.net/tokyo-disneyland-guide

Michela. (2023, June 13). *Climbing Mount Fuji: My experience and useful information*. WarmCheapTrips. https://warmcheaptrips.com/en/climbing-mount-fuji-experience-information

Miller, V. (2023, December 7). *Japan's best matsuri (festivals)*. Boutique Japan. https://boutiquejapan.com/best-japanese-festivals

Mitsui Garden Hotel Yokohama Minatomirai Premier. (n.d.). Booking.com. https://www.booking.com/hotel/jp/mitsui-garden-yokohama-minatomirai-premier.html

Miura, G. (2022, December 22). *A journey into Akita's unique rugged Oga Peninsula*. Tokyo Weekender. https://www.tokyoweekender.com/travel/oga-peninsula-akita-japan

Miyazaki, H. (Director). (1988). *My Neighbor Totoro* [Film]. Walt Disney Pictures; Troma Entertainment; Toho Co., Ltd.

Miyazaki, H. (Director). (1997). *Princess Mononoke*. Toho Co., Ltd.; Miramax.

Miyazaki, H. (Director). (2001). *Spirited Away* [Film]. Walt Disney Pictures; Toho Co., Ltd.; StudioCanal UK.

Moliere. (n.d.). Tripadvisor. https://www.tripadvisor.ca/Restaurant_Review-g298560-d4021864-Reviews-Moliere-Sapporo_Hokkaido.html

Mount Aso. (n.d.). Ervaar Japan. https://www.ervaarjapan.nl/reisgids/kyushu/kumamoto/mount-aso

Mount Misen. (n.d.). Japan-Guide.com. https://www.japan-guide.com/e/e3451.html

Mount Rokko. (n.d.). Japan-Guide.com. https://www.japan-guide.com/e/e3557.html

Mt. Aso Nakadake Crater. (n.d.). Kyushu Online Media Center. https://www.visit-kyushu.com/en/see-and-do/spots/mt-aso-nakadake-crater

Mt. Daisen. (n.d.). Japan National Tourism Organization (Official Site). https://www.japan.travel/en/spot/942

Mt. Fuji climbing guide. (n.d.). Japan National Tourism Organization. https://www.japan.travel/en/fuji-guide/mt-fuji-climbing-guide

Nagamachi Samurai District. (n.d.). Japan-Guide.com. https://www.japan-guide.com/e/e4204.html

Nagasaki Kunchi. (n.d.). Japan National Tourism Organization. https://www.japan.travel/en/spot/343

Nagasaki Kunchi Festival. (n.d.). Japan-Guide.com. https://www.japan-guide.com/e/e4411.html

Nagasaki Peace Park. (n.d.-a). Japan-Guide.com. https://www.japan-guide.com/e/e4400.html

Nagasaki Peace Park. (n.d.-b). Japan National Tourism Organization. https://www.japan.travel/en/spot/742

Naha Tug-of-War Festival 2024. (n.d.). JapanTravel. https://en.japantravel.com/okinawa/naha-tug-of-war-festival/50199

Naoshima Island. (n.d.-a). Japan-Guide.com. https://www.japan-guide.com/e/e5475.html

Naoshima Island. (n.d.-b). Japan National Tourism Organization. https://www.japan.travel/en/spot/220

Nara. (n.d.). Japan-Guide.com. https://www.japan-guide.com/e/e2165.html

Narusawa Ice Cave. (n.d.). Japan National Tourism Organization. https://www.japan.travel/en/spot/201

Naruto Strait. (n.d.). Japan Travel Planner. https://www.ana.co.jp/en/ca/japan-travel-planner/tokushima/0000001.html

Naruto whirlpools. (n.d.). Tokushima Prefectural Government. https://www.pref.tokushima.lg.jp/en/japanese/tourism/spot/uzushio

Nest Hotel Sapporo Ekimae. (n.d.). Booking.com. https://www.booking.com/hotel/jp/nest-sapporo-ekimae.en-gb.html

Nijō-jō overview. (n.d.). Discover Kyoto. https://www.discoverkyoto.com/places-go/nijo-jo

Nixy Lea. (2024). *Don't make these 3 mistakes in Hokkaido, Japan!* [Video]. YouTube. https://www.youtube.com/watch?v=cYwzyLlggqc

Noboribetsu Onsen | Travel Japan -. (n.d.). Japan National Tourism Organization. https://www.japan.travel/en/spot/1907

O'Donnell, J. (2017a, March 13). *10 Mistakes People Make Planning a Trip to Japan - J-En Translations*. J-En Translations. https://j-entranslations.com/10-mistakes-planning%E2%80%8B-a-trip-to-japan

O'Donnell, J. (2017b, March 22). *10 mistakes people make planning a trip to Japan*. LinkedIn. https://www.linkedin.com/pulse/10-mistakes-people-make-planning-trip-japan-jennifer-o-donnell?trk=public_profile_article_view

Oboke Gorge. (n.d.). Japan-Guide.com. https://www.japan-guide.com/e/e7831.html

Observation deck admission fee and business hours. (n.d.). Sapporo TV Tower. https://www.tv-tower.co.jp/en/pricetime.html

Observe some of the biggest and fastest whirlpools in the world. (n.d.). Japan National Tourism Organization. https://www.japan.travel/en/japans-local-treasures/naruto-strait-whirlpools

Odori Park. (n.d.). Japan-Guide.com. https://www.japan-guide.com/e/e5301.html

Oirase Gorge. (n.d.). Amazing Aomori. https://aomori-tourism.com/en/spot/detail_339.html

Oirase Stream. (n.d.). Japan-Guide.com. https://www.japan-guide.com/e/e3775.html

Okinawa Churaumi Aquarium. (n.d.). Japan National Tourism Organization. https://www.japan.travel/en/spot/581

Oku-Iya Kazurabashi Bridges. (n.d.). Japan-Guide.com. https://www.japan-guide.com/e/e7829.html

Oni no Sumika. (n.d.). Booking.com. https://www.booking.com/hotel/jp/xiu-shan-si-li-resu-gui-noqi.en-gb.html

Organization, J. N. T. (n.d.). *Kumamoto Castle Autumn Festival.* Japan National Tourism Organizatio. https://www.japan.travel/en/spot/450

Osaka. (n.d.). Japan-Guide.com. https://www.japan-guide.com/e/e2157.html

Osaka Castle (Osakajo). (n.d.). Japan-Guide.com. https://www.japan-guide.com/e/e4000.html

Oshokujidokoro Osanai. (n.d.). Tripadvisor. https://www.tripadvisor.com/Restaurant_Review-g298241-d2314105-Reviews-Oshokujidokoro_Osanai-Aomori_Aomori_Prefecture_Tohoku.html

Otaru Canal. (n.d.). Japan-Guide.com. https://www.japan-guide.com/e/e6701.html

Otaru Snow Light Path. (n.d.). Japan National Tourism Organization. https://www.japan.travel/en/spot/1853

Otaru Snow Light Path Festival. (n.d.). Japan-Guide.com. https://www.japan-guide.com/e/e6706.html

Peace Memorial Ceremony. (n.d.). The City of Hiroshima. https://www.city.hiroshima.lg.jp/site/english/115509.html

Peace Memorial Park. (n.d.). Japan-Guide.com. https://www.japan-guide.com/e/e3400.html

Petkoska, Z. (2021, March 17). *Udon noodle immersion in Japan's Kagawa Prefecture.* Tokyo Weekender. https://www.tokyoweekender.com/travel/udon-noodle-immersion-japans-kagawa-prefecture

Planning to rent a car and venturing out into the world on your own? Plan to obtain an International Driving Permit before you go. (n.d.). AAA Travel. https://www.aaa.com/vacation/idpf.html

Prices/sales locations. (n.d.). Greater Tokyo Pass. https://greater-tokyo-pass.jp/en/ticket

Protect yourself from potential risks with travel insurance. (n.d.). Japan National Tourism Organization. Retrieved March 6, 2024, from https://www.japan.travel/en/plan/travel-insurance-in-japan

Restaurant. (n.d.). The Fujiya Gohonjin. https://www.thefujiyagohonjin.com/en/restaurant

Rickman, C. (2023, October 15). *The city with the most Michelin star restaurants in the world.* Food Republic. https://www.foodrepublic.com/1419356/most-michelin-star-restaurants-tokyo

Ride the whirlpool sightseeing boat. (n.d.). Whirlpool Sightseeing Boat. https://www.uzusio.com/en/geton/#lnk_rat

Risks and dangers In Japan. (n.d.). Southern Cross Travel Insurance. https://www.scti.co.nz/travel-advice/dangers-in-japan

Ritsurin Garden. (n.d.). Tourism Shikoku. https://shikoku-tourism.com/en/see-and-do/10077

Rowthorn, C. (n.d.-a). *Arashiyama Bamboo Grove.* Inside Kyoto. https://www.insidekyoto.com/arashiyama-bamboo-grove

Rowthorn, C. (n.d.-b). *Okochi-Sanso Villa – Arashiyama.* Inside Kyoto. https://www.insidekyoto.com/okochi-sanso-villa-arashiyama

Ryokan Biyunoyado. (n.d.). Booking.com. https://www.booking.com/hotel/jp/ryokan-biyu-no-yado.en-gb.html

S.V. (2020, January 3). *The Kansai region.* Japan Experience. https://www.japan-experience.com/plan-your-trip/to-know/traveling-japan/the-kansai-region

Safety in Fukushima. (n.d.). Fukushima Travel. https://fukushima.travel/page/safety

Safety in Japan. (n.d.). Evaneos. https://www.evaneos.com/japan/holidays/essential-information/1550-safety

Sand dunes (Tottori Sakyu). (n.d.). Japan-Guide.com. https://www.japan-guide.com/e/e8102.html

Santiago Guesthouse Kyoto. (n.d.). Booking.com. https://www.booking.com/hotel/jp/santiago-guesthouse.en-gb.html

Sapporo Beer Museum. (n.d.). Japan-Guide.com. https://www.japan-guide.com/e/e5300.html

Sapporo Grand Hotel. (n.d.). Booking.com. https://www.booking.com/hotel/jp/sapporo-grand.html

Sapporo Snow Festival. (n.d.). Japan-Guide.com. https://www.japan-guide.com/e/e5311.html

Sapporo TV Tower. (n.d.). Sapporo Station. https://www.sapporostation.com/sapporo-tv-tower

Savor Japan. (2020a, June 5). *The 10 unmissable restaurants in Northern Honshu (Tohoku), February 2019.* https://savorjapan.com/contents/discover-oishii-japan/the-10-unmissable-restaurants-in-northern-honsyu-tohoku-february-2019

Savor Japan. (2020b, June 17). *The 10 unmissable restaurants in Western Honshu (Chugoku), February 2019.* https://savorjapan.com/contents/discover-oishii-japan/the-10-unmissable-restaurants-in-western-honsyu-cyugoku-february-2019

Savor Japan. (2023a, May 16). *The 10 unmissable restaurants in Kyushu, March 2019.* https://savorjapan.com/contents/discover-oishii-japan/the-10-unmissable-restaurants-in-kyushu-march-2019

Savor Japan. (2023b, October 25). *Food guide: 20 restaurants in Hokkaido to try its many delicacies.* https://savorjapan.com/contents/discover-oishii-japan/-hokkaido-from-the-oceans-delicacies-to-fresh-meat-dishes-10-restaurants-you-do-not-want-to-miss

Savor Japan. (2024, January 17). *Top 20 must-visit restaurants in Kyoto.* https://savorjapan.com/contents/discover-oishii-japan/-latest-edition-10-select-gourmet-foods-not-to-miss-in-kyoto

Scroope, C. (2021). *Etiquette.* Cultural Atlas. https://culturalatlas.sbs.com.au/japanese-culture/japanese-culture-etiquette

Seasons & climate of Japan: Tips for your trips. (2023, June 15). Att.JAPAN. https://att-japan.net/en/677-2

Sendai. (n.d.). Japan-Guide.com. https://www.japan-guide.com/e/e5150.html

Sendai Royal Park Hotel. (n.d.). Booking.com. https://www.booking.com/hotel/jp/sendai-royal-park.en-gb.html

Sensoji Temple. (n.d.). Japan-Guide.com. https://www.japan-guide.com/e/e3001.html

Shibuya Scramble Crossing: A must-see landmark in Tokyo. (2023, October 6). Go Tokyo. https://www.gotokyo.org/en/spot/78/index.html

Shikotsu-Toya National Park. (n.d.). Japan-Guide.com. https://www.japan-guide.com/e/e6735.html

Shinjuku Gyoen National Garden. (n.d.). Japan National Tourism Organization. https://www.japan.travel/en/spot/1659

Shirakawa-go and Gokayama. (n.d.). Japan-Guide.com. https://www.japan-guide.com/e/e5950.html

Shirakawago Guest House Kei. (n.d.). Booking.com. https://www.booking.com/hotel/jp/shirakawago-guest-house-kei.en-gb.html

Shiratani Unsuikyo. (n.d.). Japan-Guide.com. https://www.japan-guide.com/e/e4654.html

Shiroi Koibito Park. (n.d.). Japan-Guide.com. https://www.japan-guide.com/e/e5307.html

Shukkeien Garden. (n.d.). Japan-Guide.com. https://www.japan-guide.com/e/e3403.html

Smith, P. (n.d.). *10 Things not to Do in Tokyo.* Hotels.com. https://nl.hotels.com/go/japan/things-not-to-do-tokyo

Soma Nomaoi. (n.d.). Japan National Tourism Organization. https://www.japan.travel/en/spot/1740

Soma Nomaoi Festival. (n.d.). Fukushima Travel. https://fukushima.travel/destination/soma-nomaoi-festival/62

Sotetsu Fresa Inn Kobe Sannomiya. (n.d.). Booking.com. https://www.booking.com/hotel/jp/xiang-tie-huretusain-shen-hu-san-gong.en-gb.html

Special place of scenic beauty Ritsurin Garden. (n.d.). Visit Kagawa. https://www.my-kagawa.jp/static/en/ritsurin/special

Staff Writer. (2023, February 24). *Five Facts about Mt. Fuji.* Japan up Close. https://japanupclose.web-japan.org/spot/s20230224_1.html

Stanton, A. (Director). (2003). *Finding Nemo* [Film]. Walt Disney Pictures.

Staying safe in Japan. (n.d.). Japan National Tourism Organization. https://www.japan.travel/en/plan/emergencies

Steen, E. (2023, September 25). *Naoshima art island: The best museums, where to stay and what to do.* TimeOut. https://www.timeout.com/tokyo/travel/naoshima-art-island-the-best-museums-where-to-stay-and-what-to-do

Subway in Japan. (n.d.). Japan National Tourism Organization. https://www.japan.travel/en/plan/getting-around/subways

Sunriver Oboke. (n.d.). Booking.com. https://www.booking.com/hotel/jp/sunriver-oboke.en-gb.html

Szczepanski, K. (2019, May 6). *Key facts to know about Japan.* ThoughtCo. https://www.thoughtco.com/japan-facts-and-history-195581

Tahaney, E. (2020, May 4). *Future vacation tip: How to rent a motorcycle in Japan.* MotorTrend. https://www.motortrend.com/features/how-to-rent-motorcycle-japan-vacation-list

Tateyama Kurobe alpine route. (n.d.). Japan-Guide.com. https://www.japan-guide.com/e/e7550.html

Taxis in Japan. (n.d.). Japan National Tourism Organization. https://www.japan.travel/en/plan/getting-around/taxis

Tempura Motoyoshi. (n.d.). TABLEALL. https://www.tableall.com/restaurant/54

Tempura Uchitsu. (n.d.). TABLEALL. https://www.tableall.com/restaurant/61

Ten amazing winter activities in Hokkaido. (2021, March 17). Japan Wonder Travel Blog. https://blog.japanwondertravel.com/amazing-winter-activities-in-hokkaido-23617

Ten mistakes people make when visiting Kyoto. (n.d.). Hotels.com. https://nl.hotels.com/go/japan/mistakes-people-make-when-visiting-kyoto

The Editors of Encyclopaedia Britannica. (n.d.-a). Kyushu. In *Encyclopædia Britannica.* Retrieved March 30, 2024, from https://www.britannica.com/place/Kyushu-island-Japan

The Editors of Encyclopaedia Britannica. (n.d.-b). Okinawa. In *Encyclopædia Britannica.* Retrieved March 30, 2024, from https://www.britannica.com/place/Okinawa-prefecture-Japan

The Editors of Encyclopaedia Britannica. (n.d.-c). Shikoku. In *Encyclopædia Britannica.* Retrieved March 27, 2024, from https://www.britannica.com/place/Shikoku-island-Japan

The Editors of Encyclopædia Britannica. (n.d.-d). Tokyo. In *Encyclopædia Britannica.* Retrieved March 10, 2024, from https://www.britannica.com/place/Tokyo

The Editors of Encyclopedia Britannica. (n.d.-e). Hiroshima. In *Encyclopædia Britannica.* Retrieved March 20, 2024, from https://www.britannica.com/place/Hiroshima-Japan

The Editors of Encyclopedia Britannica. (n.d.-f). Hokkaido. In *Encyclopædia Britannica.* Retrieved March 26, 2024, from https://www.britannica.com/place/Hokkaido

The Hakata Gion Yamakasa Festival 2023 information. (n.d.). Fukuoka City Official Tourist Guide. https://gofukuoka.jp/articles/detail/0bb16984-ae53-4af1-b978-eb625a9c58c4

The Japan Alps and the North Chubu coast restaurants. (n.d.). Fodor's Travel. https://www.fodors.com/world/asia/japan/the-japan-alps-and-the-north-chubu-coast/restaurants

The Kanazawa area guide. (n.d.). Visit Kanazawa. https://visitkanazawa.jp/en/trip-ideas/detail_236.html

The Kansai region restaurants. (n.d.). Fodor's Travel. https://www.fodors.com/world/asia/japan/the-kansai-region/restaurants

The Mark Grand Hotel. (n.d.). Booking.com. https://www.booking.com/hotel/jp/rafre-saitama.en-gb.html

The Shikoku Pilgrimage. (n.d.). Henro. https://www.henro.org/shikoku-pilgrimage

The wooden stage on the cliff. (n.d.). Kiyomizu-Dera Temple. https://www.kiyomizudera.or.jp/en/learn/#MAIN_HALL

Thirteen amazing things to do on Miyajima Island. (2023, February 19). Bronwyn Townsend. https://www.bronwyntownsend.com/blog/things-to-do-miyajima-island

Thirty things (not) to do in Japan - easily avoid these embarrassing moments! (2021, January 8). Live Japan. https://livejapan.com/en/article-a0003666

Ticket price. (n.d.). Whirlpool Path. https://www.uzunomichi.jp/lang_en

Tickets. (n.d.-a). Ghibli Museum, Mitaka. Retrieved March 11, 2024, from https://www.ghibli-museum.jp/en/tickets

Tickets. (n.d.-b). World Heritage Site Nijo-Jo Castle. https://nijo-jocastle.city.kyoto.lg.jp/ticket/?lang=en

Tohoku. (n.d.). GaijinPot Travel. https://travel.gaijinpot.com/destination/tohoku

Tohoku region: Japan travel guide. (n.d.). Japan Rail Pass. https://www.jrailpass.com/blog/regions-of-japan/tohoku

Toji Temple and Kobo-ichi Market. (n.d.). Kyoto Station. https://www.kyotostation.com/toji-temple-kobo-ichi-market/

Tokyo Imperial Palace. (n.d.). Japan-Guide.com. https://www.japan-guide.com/e/e3017.html

Tokyo National Museum. (n.d.). Japan-Guide.com. https://www.japan-guide.com/e/e3054_tokyo.html

Tokyo Tower. (n.d.). Japan-Guide.com. https://www.japan-guide.com/e/e3009.html

Tonkatsu Keita, the hidden gem of Nishi Ogikubo. (n.d.). Tokyo Table Trip. https://tokyotabletrip.com/en/468

Tosagyoen. (n.d.). Booking.com. https://www.booking.com/hotel/jp/tosagyoen.en-gb.html

Tour of Japan: 10 Kanto regional facts. (2022, March 4). Nihongo Master. https://www.nihongomaster.com/blog/10-kanto-regional-facts

Towada-Hachimantai National Park. (n.d.). Japan-Guide.com. https://www.japan-guide.com/e/e3658.html

Toyohira River Water Garden. (n.d.). Welcome to Sapporo. https://www.sapporo.travel/en/spot/facility/water_garden

Toyoko Inn Niigata Furumachi. (n.d.). Booking.com. https://www.booking.com/hotel/jp/toyoko-inn-niigata-furumachi-niigata.en-gb.html

Travel guide to Kakunodate: Akita's charming historic town featuring samurai residences & weeping cherry blossoms. (2024, February 20). Live Japan Perfect Guide. https://livejapan.com/en/in-tohoku/in-pref-akita/in-akita-suburbs/article-a3000262

Treasure Hall. (n.d.). Miyajima Tourist Association. https://www.miyajima.or.jp/english/spot/spot_homotsukan.html

tsunagu japan_af. (2023, October 16). *9 best ryokan inns in Japan's Chugoku region for hot spring baths.* Tsunagu Japan. https://www.tsunagujapan.com/10-hot-spring-inns-chugoku-region

Uchiko. (n.d.). Japan-Guide.com. https://www.japan-guide.com/e/e5550.html

Uchiko. (n.d.). Japan National Tourism Organization. https://www.japan.travel/en/spot/4

Udon Chiyoshi. (n.d.). Tripadvisor. https://www.tripadvisor.ca/Restaurant_Review-g298138-d7379927-Reviews-Udon_Chiyoshi-Tottori_Tottori_Prefecture_Chugoku.html

Ueno Park. (n.d.). Japan-Guide.com. https://www.japan-guide.com/e/e3019.html

Understanding and mastering Japanese manners and etiquette. (n.d.). Japan National Tourism Organization. https://www.japan.travel/en/guide/understanding-and-mastering-japanese-manners-and-etiquette

Universal Studios Japan. (n.d.). Japan-Guide.com. https://www.japan-guide.com/e/e4021.html

Usuzan Ropeway. (n.d.). Japan-Guide.com. https://www.japan-guide.com/e/e6726.html

Visiting information. (n.d.). Ministry of Environment. https://www.env.go.jp/garden/shinjukugyoen/english/2_guide/guide.html

Visiting Kinkaku-ji In Kyoto – everything you need to know. (2022, October 13). Navigatio. https://thenavigatio.com/kinkakuji-kyoto-golden-pavilion-travel-tips

Visiting temples and shrines. (n.d.). Japan-Guide.com. https://www.japan-guide.com/e/e2057.html

Visitor guide: Opening times of buildings and precincts. (n.d.). Zenkoji Temple. Retrieved March 14, 2024, from https://www.zenkoji.jp/en/guide

Wada House. (2022, May 14). Shirakawa-Go Tourist Information. https://www.vill.shirakawa.lg.jp/1484.htm

Walking the Nakasendo. (2023, November 9). Go Nagano. https://www.go-nagano.net/en/trip-idea/id16492

Wanderlog Staff. (2023, July 20). *The 50 best restaurants to have dinner in Shikoku.* Wanderlog. https://wanderlog.com/list/geoCategory/375578/best-restaurants-to-have-dinner-in-shikoku

Whirlpools. (n.d.). Japan-Guide.com. https://www.japan-guide.com/e/e7852.html

Winter illuminations. (n.d.). Japan-Guide.com. https://www.japan-guide.com/e/e2304.html

Yakushima. (n.d.). Japan-Guide.com. https://www.japan-guide.com/e/e4650.html

Yakushima Island (UNESCO). (n.d.). Japan National Tourism Organization. https://www.japan.travel/en/world-heritage/yakushima-island/

Yakusugi Land. (n.d.). Japan-Guide.com. https://www.japan-guide.com/e/e4655.html

Yatsusankan. (n.d.). Booking.com. https://www.booking.com/hotel/jp/yatsusankan.en-gb.html

Yong, C. (2024, January 14). *255 useful Japanese travel words and phrases (with Kanji!).* WanderWisdom. https://wanderwisdom.com/travel-destinations/255-Useful-Travel-Japanese-Words

Yubatake (Hot Water Field). (n.d.). Japan-Guide.com. https://www.japan-guide.com/e/e7401.html

Yufuin. (n.d.). Japan-Guide.com. https://www.japan-guide.com/e/e4750.html

Yufuin Onsen. (n.d.). Japan National Tourism Organization. https://www.japan.travel/en/spot/707

Yufuin Onsen Tsukanoma. (n.d.). Booking.com. https://www.booking.com/hotel/jp/you-bu-yuan-wen-quan-shu-nojian.en-gb.html

Yufuin: 10 things to do beyond hot springs! Cafes, art, and food. (2023, December 20). Matcha. https://matcha-jp.com/en/7356#yufuin_2

Zenkoji Temple. (n.d.-a). Japan-Guide.com. https://www.japan-guide.com/e/e6001.html

Zuiganji Temple. (n.d.-b). Japan-Guide.com. https://www.japan-guide.com/e/e5102.html

Made in United States
North Haven, CT
05 November 2024

59885395R00102